"What we really have here is a lone [...] the truth of a better city that he cannot find on either side of the Atlantic. He lampoons the cherished political idols that dominate our political landscape. I couldn't suppress chortles of laughter, alongside shocks of disdain and disagreement, all the while admiring Trueman's unmasking of the well-camouflaged foolishness on all points of the political spectrum. This historian-turned-pundit, with all the force of a prizefighter's left jab and right hook, leaves the left, right, and center (or *centre*) reeling on the ropes. Therefore, I heartily recommend that you read this book, but you do so at your own peril. Its intensity, as well as its pointed, provocative, and persuasive prose, will force you to look at the Vanity Fair of politics from a pilgrim's perspective. It's just possible that you, too, will begin to yearn for a better city."

—**Peter Lillback,** President of the Providence Forum

"Carl Trueman has, with this book, broken the ammonia capsule under the noses of every starry-eyed conservative Christian, in the thrall of Republicans, capitalists, Fox News, and a gospel of mere self-interest. Here is a gauntlet that will land heavily on the toes of any who dare to take it up and read. *Republocrat* slices open the pretensions of conservative American Christianity, but not to eviscerate. His purpose, sanely and boldly argued, is to call Christians to a more carefully reasoned and biblically sound pursuit of the kingdom of God. This is a pastoral book from one who is serious about the church and earnest on behalf of the business of our King."

—**T. M. Moore,** Dean of the BreakPoint Centurions Program

"As Carl Trueman points out in his witty, provocative, and deeply well-informed way, the alliance of conservative Christianity with conservative (neoliberal) politics is a circumstance of our own context in U.S. politics—neither historically nor logically necessary. Tie the faith too closely to right-wing politics, and it's no wonder that younger Christians think they have to check out of orthodoxy when they move left of center politically. Regardless of one's own views, this book will delight, frustrate, and encourage healthy discussions that we have needed to have for a long time."

—**Michael Horton,** J. Gresham Machen Professor of Systematic Theology and Apologetics, Westminster Seminary California

"The disturbing alliance of conservative theology and right-wing politics is faced head-on in this timely and brave treatment by renowned historical-theologian and social commentator Carl Trueman. Even if readers disagree with Dr. Trueman's conclusions, the sharpness of his critique should disturb the most entrenched political consciousness, particularly if the foundations of conviction are shown to have little or no biblical support. Writing in a predictably provocative and forthright manner, Trueman pulls few, if any, punches. *Republocrat* is a timely and robust assessment of a vitally important issue and a cri de coeur for a reappraisal of the conservative church's current political alliance."

—**Derek W. H. Thomas,** John E. Richards Professor of Theology, Reformed Theological Seminary

"Nothing like an outsider's eye to bring into focus the difficulty of relating conservative politics with conservative Christianity. Relating political parties and their agendas to biblical teaching has rarely been more difficult than today. In this highly readable analysis of evangelicals' tendency to relate Christian faith to conservative politics, Trueman, a Brit playing a modern-day de Tocqueville, warns against absolutizing any political/economic worldview. His best advice: Be eclectic when listening to and reading political pundits, and be thoughtfully and actively engaged in the democratic process."

—**W. Andrew Hoffecker,** Professor of Church History, Reformed Theological Seminary

"Carl Trueman is a unique individual. Only a man of his intellectual stature and personal charity would have the courage and grace to bring together the best of both the political left and the religious right in the name of Christian statesmanship. Trueman parries and thrusts against those to the left and the right of him. Like the fourth horseman of the Apocalypse, he knocks over the sacred crockery of the Tea Party, and pours down scorn and plagues on tree-hugging, femonazi, sissy liberals. If you're a pro-gun, pro-homeschooling, anti-Obama conservative who believes that it is America's duty to nuke Iran, this book will disturb you. If you're a cross-dressing, earth-worshiping, gay, atheist professor at Yale who thinks killing unborn babies is moral, this book will infuriate you. Trueman's attempt to indigenize British communitarianism within libertarian America in the name of Christian political responsibility is sheer genius. This is political ecumenism at its very best. If Trueman were running for governor on the Republocrat ticket, I'd vote for him. I'm Michael Bird. And I endorse this message!"

—**Michael F. Bird,** Highland Theological College, Scotland, and Crossway Bible College, Australia

REPUBLOCRAT

REPUBLOCRAT

CONFESSIONS OF A
LIBERAL CONSERVATIVE

CARL R. TRUEMAN

P.O. BOX 817 • PHILLIPSBURG • NEW JERSEY 08865-0817

Printed in the United States of America

Library of Congress Cataloging-in-Publication Data

Trueman, Carl R.
 Republocrat : confessions of a liberal conservative / Carl R. Trueman.
    p. cm.
 Includes bibliographical references.
 ISBN 978-1-59638-183-4 (pbk.)
 1. Christianity and politics. I. Title.
 BR115.P7T78 2010
 261.7--dc22
                            2010019590

To Peter
Living proof that friendship can extend across
the political divide.
With God, after all, everything is possible.

CONTENTS

FOREWORD
Peter A. Lillback

WHEN THE REV. Dr. Carl Trueman asked me to write the foreword to his *Republocrat: Confessions of a Liberal Conservative,* I tentatively accepted it as an honor—at least at first. As I began to think about the daunting challenge of writing such a piece, given that I've been known as a "conservative's conservative," I began to have second thoughts. Perhaps sensing a growing skepticism on my part about the wisdom and propriety of my doing so and a palpable hesitancy to take on such a precarious task, he sweetened the invitation by divulging that he also planned to dedicate his little book to me! I knew then that I had to say an emphatic yes. How could I say no to a brother who had led me to the glorious summit of Ben Nevis and stood shoulder to shoulder with me in the dark nadir of theological controversy? It was then that I wrote to Dean Trueman, telling him that I would accept the task of writing a foreword that was "suitably contemptuous"! How else could it be done? How else could a conservative celebrate an *oxymoronic* book titled *Republocrat: Confessions of a Liberal Conservative?*

So to be "suitably contemptuous," let me consider the carefully selected adjective *oxymoronic*. I do like the fact that it concludes with the word *moronic*. I let the innuendo of that word speak for itself. But do note that the word begins with *oxy*, which has the sense of "sharp," "acidulous," or "caustic." Thus the two words together connote a sharp contradiction. Words and phrases such as *sophomore* (wise-fool), *deafening silence*, *exploding peace*, and perhaps *family vacation* fall under this rubric. So does the title *Liberal Conservative*. Indeed, it takes an oxymoronic scholar to write an oxymoronic book. Let me illustrate.

Here is a man who has memorized the lyrics of Bob Dylan and Led Zeppelin, but prefers to sing only the psalms on the Lord's Day. Here's a dean who only under coercion reluctantly walks the 26.2 steps to the president's office from the dean's office for fear of being asked to do some extra work, but regularly delights in running 26.2 miles, even if it means there will be icicles hanging from his running shorts and oozing wounds from his ice-nicked ankles. Here is a scholar who relishes the writings of Karl Marx, but who is inherently, instinctively, and immutably committed to the Reformation spirit of Martin Luther and John Calvin. Here is a man who refuses to go to counseling to address these oxymoronic traits, but who nevertheless is soon psychoanalyzed by all who associate with him. And how can a man so conflicted write intelligent blog articles read all over the globe, all the while being suspicious of technology? How can such a conflicted soul fill rooms with students eager to eat donuts with the dean, and delight generous bourgeoisie donors with the alluring British accent that suffuses his penetrating and entertaining lectures, which are supercharged by that intoxicating British genius for the mother tongue?

Perhaps this composite of opposites called Dean Trueman can be explained by genetic determinism. After all, his father was a gentleman chartered public accountant, well respected in his service to the bourgeoisie leadership class in the UK. But his grandfather was a brawling union boss who busted up more than one pub to keep the proletariat workers in line. Clearly, there are reasons for the oxymoronic Trueman disposition. At least we can see why we should extend a bit of sympathy in his direction.

I gained insight about Dr. Trueman's oxymoronic spirit when we traveled to the Highgate tube stop in London to take the trek to the massive granite bust of Karl Marx that looms over his grave. I went to make sure Marx was dead, and was careful to have my photograph taken standing to the *right*, with an appropriate distance separating me from the bust. But not so Dean Trueman. Leaning on the monument that proclaims, "Workers of all lands unite," this now-ordained OPC minister was comfortably to the left of Comrade Karl. I've since been regularly tempted to misspell Dean Trueman's first name with a K—Karl Trueman. Given that his impeccable logic is almost always fatal in debate, I've even toyed with renaming him Karl Marxman.

But it's here that the danger of writing this foreword began to sink in. Perhaps by being required to read his book, I would be persuaded! For Trueman's truculent pen and lethal logic would surely have an impact. Even the dead around Marx's grave were not spared. Dean Trueman noted the absurdity of materialists seeking to be buried around Marx's tomb, with headstones adorned with foolish inscriptions such as: "With gratitude from a fellow Communist." The unyielding grave and hopeless end of Communistic materialism made such acts of homage not just illogical but tragic. Only the resurrection—emphatically denied by dialectical materialists—noted Dean Trueman, made such veneration in death have any significance.

So in agreeing to write the foreword, I also made an agreement with myself. I would write the "suitably contemptuous" part before I wrote the conclusion. I feared that I could not maintain the Erasmian spirit of *In Praise of Folly* needed to distance myself from Dean Trueman's political "liberalism" if I first submitted myself to his persuasive pen and trenchant thought. Only in this way could I take the risk of publicly embarrassing myself by becoming a neutered conservative, a sycophant of an oxymoronic scholar.

So to steel my mind, I reminded myself that Dean Trueman was not such a bad chap after all. Hadn't he given up the interminable monotony of cricket to come to the city of the world-champion Phillies? Hadn't he abandoned the wimpy kickball of the UK, I mean soccer, I mean British football, for the nation where real men play real football? Hadn't he, like the Reformed Presbyterian leader John Witherspoon, left Britain to come to the New World with his Scottish wife? How could I not embrace this challenge? He was a Westminster Seminary scholar, a theological mind formed at St. Catharine's in Cambridge, and a graduate scholar from Aberdeen.

Thus mentally prepared, I took up and read. But I did so also remembering our tour of Bunhill Fields in London—the burial grounds of nonconformists including John Bunyan, Thomas Goodwin, Oliver Cromwell's son, and others persecuted by the Anglican "conservative" establishment. This excursion had previously helped me to see why Puritan and "liberal" were historically closely linked in the British context. King Charles I certainly understood that Oliver Cromwell was no conservative in terms of British politics!

So in turning from the *ad hominem* to the *ad substantiam*, what do we learn from an actual engagement with Trueman's *Republocrat: Confessions of a Liberal Conservative*? To distill the thoughts that came to mind, a couplet not written by Dylan or Zeppelin emerged:

> Pilgrims see what locals don't
> And strangers speak when others won't.

In other words, this book is wrongly titled. It's not the *Republocrat: Confessions of a Liberal Conservative* at all. If it were that, as Dean Trueman makes abundantly clear as he begins, the title should be *Confessions of an Old Liberal Conservative*. Even better, its title should be *The Critique of Political Folly by a Pilgrim in a Strange Land*. The liberals of today, no more than the conservatives in contemporary America, can take no comfort in this jeremiad on the inane and the inept that often characterizes the popular press and media maelstrom. What we really have here is a critique, written from a deep sense of alienation, indeed, from the perspective of a political alien, an outsider, a lonely thinker who longs for the truth of a better city that he cannot find on either side of the Atlantic. His omnidirectional diatribe lampoons the cherished political idols that dominate our political landscape.

In the spirit of a good brawl, led by a union boss busting up an otherwise quiet pub, our author's criticisms take no prisoners, whether they're Marx, Marcuse, Murdoch, Major, Beck, O'Reilly, Limbaugh, the BBC, the New Left, the conservative Right, Bush, Clinton, or even *The Patriot's Bible*. (Thankfully, he leaves my hero George Washington unscathed!) Even conservative Presbyterians, automobiles, and televisions come under his shock-and-awe campaign. I must admit that even as a conservative I couldn't suppress chortles of laughter, alongside shocks of disdain and disagreement, all the while admiring Trueman's unmasking of the well-camouflaged foolishness on all points of the political spectrum.

This historian-turned-pundit, with all the force of a prize-fighter's left jab and right hook, leaves the left, right, and center (or *centre*) reeling on the ropes. But that doesn't mean that he wins the match. His opponents may fall to his wit, words, and wallop, but that doesn't mean he gets it all right. Just because Bill O'Reilly is illogical at times and Glenn Beck's histrionics are more stage than sage, that doesn't mean there aren't good reasons to avoid the socialization of medicine and the limitation of Second Amendment rights. But since I'll admit I'm a bit gun-shy—I'm writing a foreword, after all—I'll wait for a safer place to tear apart the straw men that Trueman has lurking in his arguments and the subtle non sequiturs that stalk his conclusions. One problem with Trueman's critique I cannot help but point out here: it is the vastly understated admission "I also have no problem with outrageous overstatement to make a point, no doubt being guilty of it myself on various occasions." This humble admission left me wondering whether the author had read his own book! But there is socially redeeming value in this pilgrim's pogrom against political pabulum: "Indeed, I look forward to the day when intelligence and civility, not tiresome clichés, character assassinations, and Manichaean noise, are the hallmarks of Christians as they engage the political process."

So in the spirit of that eschatological hope, I heartily recommend that you read this book. But you do so at your own peril. Its intensity, as well as its pointed, provocative, and persuasive prose, will force you to look at the Vanity Fair of politics from a pilgrim's perspective. It's just possible that you, too, will begin to yearn for a better city. And because of the grace of that city, I'm grateful that a conservative's conservative can call a liberal conservative a precious brother in Christ. Thanks so much for this great honor, Karl, I mean Carl!

Acknowledgments

I NEVER WANTED to write this book; frankly, I probably do not need the grief that its basic thesis—that religious conservatism does not demand unconditional political conservatism—could well bring to my e-mail in-box. Nevertheless, when Marvin Padgett and Ian Thompson at P&R Publishing approached me with the idea and suggested that I might be the one to do it, against my better judgment I agreed to write it. So thanks must go first to them, and then to the staff at P&R who worked so hard to take the book to press.

I must also thank Sandy Finlayson for many conversations about the issues with which I deal. As a fellow immigrant, and from a confessional church tradition that often involved social radicalism, he is a true kindred spirit; and like me, he believes there is nothing like a glass of brandy to bring clarity to a political discussion. Thanks also to Rob Burns, former student, whose knowledge of radical politics far outstrips my own, and who, in the later months of the project, was a source of encouragement and of some important information and sources on some of the matters discussed herein.

Thanks as always to the ladies in Academic Affairs—Becky, Leah, and Rebecca—who keep the office running so effectively that their boss has time to write; to the trustees at Westminster for granting me study leave, part of which I used to finish this book; and to my beloved wife, Catriona, and sons, John and Peter, for providing such a happy home.

Finally, thanks to Peter Lillback, president of Westminster Theological Seminary, for writing the foreword. Peter and I are poles apart in our political commitments, and I have often commented to him that, on paper, we should be neither friends nor colleagues; but both our friendship and our working relationship seem to work, and, indeed, to do so remarkably well. This book is dedicated to him, with the hope that it does not ruin his reputation!

Introduction

DESPITE THE TITLE of this book, I do not intend to spend much time talking about myself. Indeed, the thesis of this book—that conservative Christianity does not require conservative politics or conservative cultural agendas—is both more important and more interesting than the author. Nevertheless, I believe it is helpful to the reader to know something about me as an author, in order to understand the perspective, or bias, with which I write. For some, it will merely confirm that I am a bleeding-heart liberal; for others, just another foreigner who does not understand America; to yet more, an incoherent anomaly whose theology and politics coexist by an act of perverse will rather than by any necessary connection or mutual consistency. Indeed, some in this latter group might therefore regard me as a traitor to the great political cause of conservative Christianity—a wolf in sheep's clothing. And then, strange to tell, if any truly left-wing person happens to read what I have to say, I will probably appear to be not so liberal after all, given my position on abortion and gay marriage—ironically the two litmus tests used today to identify commitment to a truly radical agenda. What can I say? I am simply delighted that I will disappoint so many different groups of people in such a comprehensive manner. After all, a man is known by the quantity and quality of his enemies as much as, if not more than, by those of his friends.

The primary reason why I agreed to write this book is my belief that the evangelical church in America is in danger of alienating a significant section of its people, particularly younger people, through too tight a connection between conservative party politics and Christian fidelity. For example, the use of abortion as a wedge issue and as a clear dividing line between Republican and Democratic parties has the potential to kill intelligent discussion on a host of other political topics. After all, if Republican and Democrat are the only two credible electoral options in most places, then, according to many, the Christian way of voting is obvious, and it is pointless to discuss any other policies or issues.

Such an attitude is in my experience very common in Christian circles, and it is problematic for two reasons. First, it fails to address the difference between Republican rhetoric on abortion and action on the same, which is often dramatic and serves to weaken the rather stark polarities that are often drawn between Republicans and Democrats. Second, it preempts discussion on a host of other issues—poverty, the environment, foreign policy, etc.—and thereby runs the risk of provoking a reaction among younger evangelicals that relativizes the issue of abortion and thus achieves the opposite of what it intends. Sadly, there is evidence that this is already taking place in some quarters. This attitude is antithetical to Christianity as I understand it. To cite the Greek apologists, Christians are to be the best citizens, and being the best citizens requires being informed and thoughtful on a whole host of issues that impact the civic sphere. As Christians, therefore, we need above all things to think carefully about politics, to engage the process and the issues in a way that respects their complexity, and to avoid the clichés, oversimplifications, and Manichaeism that bedevil electoral campaigns.

I have always loved a political argument. As a youngster, I was passionately interested in politics, activism, and political writing. Ironically (at least from the perspective of today), I was a member of the British Conservative Party in the mid-1980s, during the heyday of Mrs. Thatcher. I voted Tory in 1987 and again in 1992. My reasons were simple: I saw the Tories as the best hope for keeping out of power a Labour Party that had been infiltrated by radical Trotskyite elements (the infamous Militant Tendency), which, although purged by the late 1980s, had left the party unfit and unprepared for government. I also thought that the Tories offered the best protection of traditional values, from those connected to the family to those embodied in education. By 1997, however, I had switched my allegiance to the Liberal Democrats, the party of the center, or perhaps center-left, in British politics. That is basically where I have remained.

My reason for the initial shift was simple: after eighteen years of Conservative rule, the corruption of the John Major government was obvious for all to see, and I am firmly of the belief that a season out of power is the best corrective to political arrogance, complacency, and corruption. Yet there was more to my shift than the simple pragmatics of party politics in a democracy. I had also come to a general realization that Thatcher had pulled off something of a political balancing act that was now clearly no longer viable: she had married free-market economics to traditional values, and built an electable party on the basis of an alliance of supporters of these two positions; but as I will argue in a later essay in this book, such an alliance was always doomed to be inherently unstable and in the long run unviable.

My leftward turn was confirmed and solidified, however, by an event that took place in China—or, rather, did not take place in China. Hong Kong was, until 1997, a British colony; when the lease expired, it was handed back to the Chinese. The last governor of the colony was a former minister in the Thatcher government, Chris Patten. He used his time in Hong Kong to fight as hard as he could to make sure it would retain as many of its democratic freedoms and institutions as it had enjoyed under British rule. Of course, the task was doomed from the start: the Chinese were interested in having Hong Kong back for cultural and economic reasons, but they had no intention of allowing anything approaching a Western democracy to remain in place.

After the handover, Patten wrote his memoirs, which were to be published by HarperCollins. They were, however, pulled from publication by that company after the owner, Rupert Murdoch, intervened. The reason? Murdoch seemed to think that his business interests in China would be damaged by the book, with its revelations of how the Chinese had acted in the buildup to the handing over of power.[1]

To understand the shock this was to a young conservative, one must understand something of what it was like to grow up in Europe in the 1970s and 1980s, and the role Rupert Murdoch played in that. The Soviet Union loomed large; the fear of nuclear confrontation, while never imminent, was always lurking in the background; and

1. See the report at http://news.bbc.co.uk/2/hi/world/analysis/61122.stm. Accessed 1/19/2010.

tales of restrictions on freedom behind the Iron Curtain seemed too much like a taste of what might be coming our way. In this context, Thatcher's robust anti-Communism was important; and the demands of the Murdoch press, through men such as *Sunday Times* Editor Andrew Neill, for freedom of speech, combined with vigorous opposition to totalitarian politicians at home and abroad, seemed to represent a significant stand for liberty.

All this, of course, changed when HarperCollins blackballed Patten's memoirs at the apparent request of the owner, Mr. Murdoch. Suddenly, the great opponent of Communist totalitarianism did not appear to be such a champion of liberty and freedom of speech after all. In fact, he seemed more like an opportunist with a sharp eye for a business deal than an idealist. Furthermore, his action relative to China now raised doubts in my mind concerning his earlier opposition to the Soviet Union. Was it really lack of freedom to which he had been opposed? Or was it rather the fact that the Soviets had closed their markets to his products?

This anecdote may be new to many readers; it probably did not even make the inside pages of the news in the USA, but for me it was a watershed. And of course, Murdoch is the owner not only of HarperCollins, but of Fox News, the channel of choice for many conservative Christians in the USA and a channel to which we will be returning in subsequent pages of this book.

The next stage of my political transformation was my move to the USA in 2001. Emigration can be a vertiginously disorienting experience at the best of times, and the fact that America and Britain share (approximately) the same language does little to defuse this effect. Indeed, it may actually intensify the confusion in some ways, since the immigrant's naive expectation that everything in the new country will approximate to the old leads inevitably to a greater feeling of dislocation. I had lived in America for six months in 1996, and so was familiar with the culture a little more than the typical tourist; but still I was not fully prepared for many of the differences—from the execrable (cheese from an aerosol can) to the delightful (restaurant meals that did not break the bank) and all points in between. Most noticeable for me at a philosophical level, however, was that I suddenly found myself to be a man of the left. I had always regarded myself as essentially a centrist, drifting sometimes a little right, sometimes a little left of the midpoint in political ideology, but certainly no radical of dangerously deviant and subversive views.

I was rapidly disabused of my self-image as a moderate. On one of my very first Sundays in the USA, I was engaged in a conversation with a friend over coffee after church, and mentioned in passing what great work I thought the Clintons had done in Ulster. I might as well have said that Jack the Ripper had really helped to make the streets of London safe for women and children. I was given the full forty-minute "truth about Billary" lecture, and left the building in no doubt that the Clintons were, after Hitler, Stalin, and Pol Pot, probably the most dangerous and wicked leaders in the history of world politics. I had just learned an important lesson: American politics is Manichaean, about an elemental struggle between good and evil where, as in those 1940s B-Westerns, the goodies are as obvious as the men in white hats, and the baddies stand out because of their invariable preference for black headgear. Good deeds done by the baddies in one area are simply clever ruses to hide the real agenda of wickedness being pursued in another, and stupid foreigners like me are simply not equipped to discern the depth of the conspiracy we are up against.

It is against this dual background that this little book is written: first, my own disillusion with the Right and subsequent move to centrist political commitments (and I mean *centrist* in the British sense—that's "left" to Americans and "right" to Hugo Chavez), and second, my concern that the identification of Christianity with political agendas, whether of the right or the left, is problematic for a variety of reasons. Much of my immediate concern is with the Religious Right, because the USA is my adopted context and the Religious Right is where I see the most immediate problem. But hard-and-fast identification of gospel faithfulness with the Left, or even with the center, can be just as problematic. The gospel cannot and must not be identified with partisan political posturing.

I might also add that as a foreigner I suspect that I defy neat categorization in the simple taxonomy of religious politics in the USA. Being pro-life and anti-gay marriage, I would hardly be welcome on the secular left of the spectrum. In favor of gun control and nationalized health care, I doubt that I am ever going to be made an honorary life member of the Cato Institute. I also look to writers and thinkers from all parts of the political spectrum. William Hazlitt, George Orwell, Arthur Koestler, Edward Said, Alexander Solzhenitsyn, Terry Eagleton, Nat Hentoff, P. J. O'Rourke, Christopher Hitchens, John Lukacs, Charles Moore, Roger Scruton—these writers span the left-right divide, and yet I have enjoyed and profited from them all. Of particular importance to me have been the writings of Orwell and also Koestler's stunning masterpiece, *Darkness at Noon*, for the way they exposed the psychology of the totalitarian mind-set and pointed to the necessity of freedom of speech as basic to a free society. Indeed, perhaps what all of these writers have in common is a certain independent radicalism—none of them quite fit the stereotypes associated with their own chosen political affiliations; and that, perhaps, is what is most appealing about them. Their writings do not conform but rather show that the writers thought for themselves in ways that were neither hackneyed and mindlessly partisan nor driven by sound bites and clichés.

The following pages mark my attempt, slight as it is, to stand in their shoes relative to my own adopted constituency—the religiously conservative world of American Protestant Christianity. While there is a certain amount of cross-referencing, the chapters do not form a particularly sustained and sequential argument, but can be read in isolation, as snapshot reflections upon the connection between the Christian religion and politics as I see it in my own life in the USA context. My purpose is merely to show that the situation should not be as simple as the gurus of the Religious Right or their opponents on the secular Left seek to make it. Indeed, the overall thesis of this book is not so much a political one; rather, it can be summed up as "Politics in democracy is a whole lot more complicated than either political parties or your pastor tell you it is; treat it as such—learn about the issues and think for yourself."

This is why it is strangely appropriate for a trained historian, rather than a philosopher, to write this little book. The task of the historian, as one of my good historian friends often says, is to make things more complicated. I am reasonably sure that committed conservative Christians for whom politics is almost as important as theology will see this book as a tract for the Left—little more than the special pleading of a confused political liberal who cannot see the connection between his religious beliefs and his political commitments. To such people I will be a disappointment. I suspect the same will, ironically, be the case with any of the secular Left who happen to thumb these pages (unlikely, I know, but possible). To them, I will be woefully inconsistent, having a concern for the environment and poverty but opposing women's rights (in the form of abortion) and oppressing minorities (in the form of opposition to gay marriage); to them I will not be a man of the Left but merely an inconsistent bigot of the Right. I trust I am neither; in fact, I hope that I am a bit more complicated and a bit less confused than either interpretation. But that is for the reader to decide.

LEFT BEHIND

A CHAPTER ARGUING that the Left has lost its way and is barely worthy of support these days seems a suitably contrarian place to begin this book, and something that will at least offer temporary relief to those who fear the work as a whole is simply going to be a diatribe against the Right. On the contrary, this book is not intended as a plea for one party or one political philosophy over another. It is rather a plea for seeing the situation as more complicated and less black-and-white than is often the case in Christian circles.

This first chapter really sets the background for my own approach to the issues. As a Christian, I believe that many of the things that I consider important were embodied in the original vision of what I might call old-style, just-left-of-center politics. Sadly, the things I hold dear as important political issues—poverty, sanitation, housing, unemployment, hunger—have, from the 1950s onward, been eclipsed by a new set of Left concerns that have little to do with the kind of social liberalism and aspirations to equality of opportunity to which I thought the Left was committed. The result is that the Left has been hijacked by special-interest groups, and is frequently less concerned than even the parties of the Right with those for whom it should really speak up. That leaves people such as me with no political place to call home. To put it bluntly, we have been left behind.

A BRIEF HISTORY OF THE OLD LEFT

Anyone who spends any time reflecting on the history of political activism will very soon realize that the Left of today bears little or no resemblance to that of the nineteenth century. The rise of the political Left in Europe took place as a response to the dramatic social changes surrounding the Industrial Revolution. As factories and production became the centerpieces of economies in places such as Britain, urban populations experienced exponential growth, workforces expanded, and a struggle inevitably ensued among the old landed aristocracies, the new factory owners and tradesmen, and the workforces that provided the raw labor to make the whole thing possible. In the cities, slums expanded, child labor became an issue, and everywhere poverty and hardship were visible. Nor was the countryside immune: the shift of population and economic emphasis to urban industrial centers had a negative impact on agricultural workers who remained in the countryside.

This provides the background to much of the rise of the Left. In nineteenth-century Britain, the Industrial Revolution provided the dynamic to some of the most significant legislation of the time.

This itself bears witness to the growing power of those outside the traditional aristocracy, which, until then, had enjoyed a virtual monopoly when it came to political power. Thus, for example, in 1824–25 the British Parliament repealed the Combination Acts, effectively making it legal for trade unions to organize. Then, in 1832, the Reform Act extended, but did not universalize, the franchise. These moves were in some sense pretty paltry, but they clearly indicate that Britain was slowly but surely moving toward what we now recognize as a modern democratic state and, more importantly, that the powers that be were being forced to acknowledge that society was changing in previously unimaginable ways.

Trade unions and organized labor were one form of response to the growing needs of workers in the nineteenth century. At another level, various social philosophers articulated political and economic philosophies designed to address the new shape of society and the problems that were being generated for the poor by the dramatic changes taking place. These philosophies varied in terms of how radical their proposals were; for sure, not all such responses could be characterized as "Left." In Britain, Thomas Chalmers, a leader of the Evangelical Party in the Church of Scotland, was horrified as a young pastor by the slums he found in his parish in Glasgow, to which his response was a system of parish visitation and diaconal care. Yet Chalmers remained a High Tory, and like Jane Austen's Emma, his concern for the poor was driven by a sense of *noblesse oblige* and paternalism. Others, however, were articulating more radical approaches to the problem.

The most famous of the truly radical responses to the problems of industrialization were the writings of Karl Marx. Marx, a German-born Jew, was profoundly influenced by the philosophical school that stemmed from the work of G. W. F. Hegel. Hegel had argued that the whole of history should be conceived of as a great unfolding of dialectical tension; but where Hegel saw this unfolding in intellectual or, perhaps better, spiritual terms, Marx turned Hegel's thinking on its head and rooted this historical dynamic in materialism, specifically the movement of capital and the power relations that connected to this. For Marx, history moved through a series of phases—from a rural feudalism, where an aristocracy essentially held power and sat at the top of the social ladder, through a period of bourgeois control, where power passed to the hands of those who owned the means of production (i.e., factories), distribution (traders), and capital (bankers), to a future utopian state where the workers themselves would control the fruits of their labor. At this point history, in terms of the development of social relations, would come to an end. The whole scheme was inevitable and unavoidable—the workers would triumph.

The many flaws in Marx's theories have been demonstrated countless times over the last century, both in scholarly critiques and, more brutally, in the failed economies, totalitarianism, and gulags that seem an essential part of the Marxist project when put into practice. Marx is interesting to us at this point, however, because his theories, although the most radical in their location of class conflict as the driving force of history, still provide a good indication of what the Left considered important, at least in its inception.

For Marx, as for most of what I might call here the "Old Left," as opposed to the "New Left" that emerged as a force in the 1960s, the major concern was with oppression: how are people oppressed, and what can or should be done about it? For Marx, history held the answer: eventually there would be revolution, and the middle classes would be toppled from power by the working classes. For others on the Left, more constitutional means were to be employed: trade unions, political parties, a broadened franchise, a welfare state, etc. All of these could be used to deal with the issue of oppression. The analysis of the situation varied, as did the proposed solutions, but they all had one basic thing in common: they saw oppression as primarily an economic issue, something empirically observable. Some people possessed more than others, and some did not enjoy either the material goods or the working conditions to allow them to live with any quality of life. This was the problem the various movements on the Left wished to address. The philosophies varied, but there was basic agreement on the problem: economic poverty.

THE STRANGE LOVE AFFAIR OF THE INTELLIGENTSIA WITH MARXISM

At first glance, it is perplexing to look back on the twentieth century and see how many intellectuals from Western, liberal democracies were fooled by the promises and rhetoric of Marxism; but this is perhaps more explicable when we look at the context. In the course of history, Communism received something of a boost from the Russian Revolution of 1917, which seemed to indicate that Marxism, at least in its modified, Leninist form, was indeed correct in its claims about the way history was moving. That the revolution had started in an agrarian, rather than industrial, society was odd and involved Lenin and Trotsky, the Revolution's theorists, in certain revisions of Marxist theory; but the rapid industrialization of Russia in the subsequent decades seemed only to prove the superiority of the Marxist cause over its socialist and capitalist rivals. Only later was the appalling human cost of Soviet industrialization to be revealed to the wider world.

A second element that added to the appeal of Marxism to the Left at this point was, paradoxically, the rise of Fascism and Nazism. It is often staggering to look back to the 1930s and see how many intellectuals—George Bernard Shaw, Arthur Koestler, H. G. Wells, Stephen Spender, and many others—were taken in by the ideology of the Soviet Union. Some of these intellectuals, including Koestler and Spender, were later to repudiate the creed and write devastatingly against it. Today, post-1956, 1968, and 1989, this commitment seems utterly bizarre; but in the 1930s, the full extent of the butchery of Lenin and Stalin was not yet known, and Communism seemed to provide the only vigorous and compelling opposition to the hard Right vision of the Mussolinis, Hitlers, Francos, and Codreanus. Fascism and Communism grew together in a kind of vicious symbiosis. To those opposed to Nazism, it seemed Marxism offered the last, best hope—until, of course, the Nazi-Soviet Pact of 1939; although even after that, many hung on to the illusions of Marxism until the 1956 Hungarian Revolution and beyond. It was a sorry case of never mind the facts, give me the romantic vision.

SUCCESS AND FAILURE: THE ROAD TO REDEFINITION

Beyond the narrow bounds of Marxism, the history of Britain in the first half of the twentieth century bears witness to many successes of the Left with regard to the Old Left issues of political and economic oppression. The universal franchise was granted in 1928, and the foundations of the welfare state were laid in the Liberal governments of the first two decades of the century, reaching full expression with the founding of the National Health Service during the Labor government of Clement Attlee of 1945. To those who have a knee-jerk reaction against government health schemes, I am one who probably owes his very existence to such a scheme: the system basically provided my maternal grandparents with health care that would otherwise have been impossible to obtain; and for the record, they were far from the welfare scroungers so beloved of certain types of conservative political pundits. Grand-dad worked in a factory, Grandma scrubbed floors, and neither was ever in debt. They were just poor—hardworking but poor. In the world of the late 1940s and early 1950s, some form of mixed economy, with a moderate welfare provision, seemed the best way to alleviate such poverty.

If the first half of the twentieth century seemed to point toward some form of socialism as the wave of the future, the second half put the lie to that notion. On the far Left, a series of crises demonstrated beyond question the vicious effects of totalitarian Communism. The gulags of Stalin's Soviet Union, the suppression of the Hungarian Revolution and the Prague Spring, the Cultural Revolution in China, the killing fields of Cambodia, to name but a few, showed how the quest for utopia so often ends in a blood-soaked nightmare, whose victims are the very poor and oppressed for whom the Left professes to be most concerned. Then the collapse of the Soviet Union and its satellites, symbolized above all by the fall of the Berlin Wall, indicated that the Communist experiment, at least in its Soviet form, was at an end. While Cuba limped on, and China chose a very different path, mainstream Communism of the classical variety was dead.

While the hard Left was in disarray in the totalitarian regimes of Eastern Europe, the intellectual hard Left of the West had also undergone something of a transformation. I noted above how the Left, for all its diversity on economic issues, originally exhibited a consensus on what constituted the primary form of oppression: it was economic, and involved some people possessing control over things important to quality of life that others lacked. For example, John Doe had fresh running water but fenced off his spring so that Fred Bloggs and his family could not get access to it; Pete Smith insisted on selling his apples at a price that most poor people could not afford; and so on and so forth.

By the 1950s, however, it was becoming clear to a number of Left intellectuals that the long-awaited world revolution was probably not going to come and that the revolutions that had arrived had not produced quite the unequivocal utopias that had been expected. Alongside this, the collapse of the old nineteenth-century European empires after the Second World War, and the rise of nationalist movements in the former imperial colonies, had added new dimensions to notions of liberation. Ethnicity, for example, as much as economics, now started to play a role. In retrospect, it is clear that ethnicity was always a factor, perhaps often a more significant factor than economic class, even in Communist revolutions. But now movements of ethnic liberation became explicitly linked to left-wing ideology, of which the struggle against apartheid in South Africa is perhaps the best known. This was in some ways an odd move; it represented a subtle shift away from oppression seen in purely economic terms (though ethnic oppression typically involves economic oppression). Moreover, with its explicit nationalist and ethnic interests, it exhibited some affinities with earlier right-wing movements.

MR. MARX MEETS DR. FREUD: THE CHANGING FACE OF OPPRESSION

In addition to the nationalist-left alliance at a practical level, a possibly even more significant alliance was occurring at an intellectual level. In the 1950s and 1960s, the work of a number of Marxist cultural critics, associated with an intellectual group known as the Frankfurt School (because its primary advocates were based at the Institute for Social Research at the University of Frankfurt am Main in what was then West Germany), began to take root. The Frankfurt School was responsible for development of so-called critical theory, which represented an attempt to articulate a future for Marxist-based social change in a way that offered an alternative to both Western liberal democracy and the Stalinism of the Soviet Union. Crucial to the popular politics of the Left was the fusion that certain leaders of the school, most notably Herbert Marcuse, achieved between classical Marxism and Freudianism.

Supplementing the economic categories of Marx with the psychoanalytic categories of Freud, Marcuse and his followers effectively broadened the whole notion of oppression to include the psychological realm. Such a move is dramatic in the implications it has for the way one views politics. Simply put, oppression ceases to be something that can be assessed empirically in terms of external economic conditions and relations, and becomes something rather more difficult to see, i.e., a matter of the psychology of social relations. Marcuse's particular concern was the impact of consumerism, the acquisition of material goods, on the individual. The market gave individuals an illusion of freedom, in that they thought they had choice over what they bought. But in fact the kinds of goods available were limited by what the people in charge chose to sell, and the driving forces of the market—advertising, commercials, etc.—were simply a form of propaganda that tricked people into thinking they needed particular goods in order to be happy. The poor, benighted public was the victim of a manipulative capitalism that first created wants and then satisfied them. Thus oppression was psychologized. No longer was it lack of material goods that constituted oppression; now oppression was essentially defined as being tricked into thinking that material goods were the answer.

One can see in the work of Marcuse and company a response to an awkward fact that was becoming increasingly obvious in the 1950s and 1960s. The problem that Marxist intellectuals faced was this: they wanted a workers' revolution that would usher in the proletarian utopia, but in the boom years after World War II, it became increasingly obvious that the working class did not want a workers' utopia; they wanted to own consumer goods. They didn't want workers' councils; they wanted cars, televisions, washing machines, and countless other things. The accumulation of "stuff," not the reorganization of the means of production, was what motivated them. I well remember walking around one of the poorer estates in Aberdeen some years ago and noticing that the number of large, ostentatious satellite dishes attached to the housing blocks seemed to far outstrip anything I ever saw on the middle-class street where I lived. The opium of the people, one might say, was no longer religion; rather, it was televised entertainment. People did not want the vote; they wanted soap operas on demand.

Seen in this light, Marcuse's work can be interpreted as a response to the rise of the consumer society; and the political problem of human existence was not poverty so much as inauthenticity—the making of men and women into what they were not designed to be, which consumerism brought into being. It also helped to explain, from the perspective of the Left, why conservative leaders such as Ronald Reagan and Margaret Thatcher proved so popular: they facilitated the consumer society and even appealed across traditional class boundaries. They offered not true, authentic freedom, as Marcuse understood it; they offered the one-dimensional existence of a society that saw meaning in mere material accumulation—the modern equivalent of the Roman bread-and-circuses strategy.

HOW AUTHENTICITY MADE THE LEFT INAUTHENTIC

The significance of this move by the Left can hardly be overestimated. By placing notions such as *authenticity* at the center of its agenda, the Left was able to broaden its set of concerns far beyond the mere economic or political in the traditional sense of the word. Indeed, it is arguable that the economic and material concerns that drove the radicals of the nineteenth and early twentieth centuries virtually vanished, to be replaced by a whole set of much more contentious and nebulous issues. Now, with "authenticity" being the goal, and that conceived of in psychological terms, oppression itself was psychologized so that even the person who enjoyed good material conditions might yet be "inauthentic" because of the way in which society imposed its values upon him or her. Oppression takes place inside the head, as individuals are manipulated and kept quiescent by the forces of mass media and a surfeit of goods and possessions. Cynically, one might say that oppression becomes whatever the Left intellectuals say it is or whatever the lobby groups decide to campaign against.

Such an approach easily combined with a number of other impulses within the wider intellectual culture. Postcolonial thought, with its emphasis on debunking any notion that Western democratic institutions and values were essential goods, argued rather that such things were simply the latest stage of the attempts of the Western powermongers to impose their will and values on the rest of the world. Then, various strands of postmodernism offered critiques of values within Western society itself, particularly in terms of sexual mores and gender roles. To make heterosexuality and monogamous marriage normative was, again, oppressive and prevented the gays, lesbians, and others who might have once been regarded as deviant from being "authentic."

This psychologizing of oppression, combined with postcolonial thinking and postmodernism, has led the organized Left to adopt some strange positions that once would have been antithetical to its philosophy. For example, it has often been the case that the most intolerant groups with regard to homosexuality are working-class; the issue of gay rights is, by and large, the preoccupation of the middle class. So in advocating gay rights, the Left frequently finds itself opposed to the values of the very people it was originally designed to help.

Further, while the Left in origin was supposed to provide a voice to the voiceless, the link that has been forged between abortion and women's rights has meant that the most voiceless of all—the unborn—are those most vigorously silenced by those who should be speaking for them. This irony and moral inconsistency has not always been lost on those who would regard themselves as being of the political Left and, in the case of a man such as Nat Hentoff, helped to convert him to the pro-life cause. The anomaly is most embarrassingly obvious at international congresses on women's rights, where women from poorer countries who struggle daily with issues such as clean water, food, female circumcision, etc., often seem bemused by the obsession of the materially well-off women of the West with the matter of abortion. This hijacking of the Left by identity politics means that the current struggles in which the Left are engaged are not of a kind that my grandfather would have recognized, and represent rather a betrayal of the Old Left.

Then, of course, the most obvious problems occur with wars and international relations. Growing up in the 1970s and 1980s, I could never quite understand why the Right wanted a boycott of the 1980 Olympics over the Soviet invasion of Afghanistan, but opposed sporting bans on South Africa, while the Left was outraged at any attempt to boycott the Olympics, because "politics should be kept out of sport," yet reviled any sports person who had contact with South Africa. The answer, of course, was that neither side was really concerned about freedom; it was more about which regime was more acceptable. That the Left thought the world of Brezhnev and company—most of whom had blood on their hands from rising under Stalin, not to mention their subsequent involvement in repression—somehow better than the world of Vorster and Botha was ridiculous, but it showed how far they had come from original ideals of human rights.

Yet the situation today is, if anything, worse. The Left's opposition to the wars in Afghanistan and Iraq is odd, given that both represented feudal regimes with despicable records on human rights. That the regimes were nasty and vicious does not justify an outside power invading sovereign territory; but to listen to much of the rhetoric on the Left and to see the craven obeisance paid to a man like Saddam Hussein by a so-called man of the Left like British MP George Galloway is sickening. The Left was supposed to be committed to speaking up against oppression *wherever* it may be found, not simply in those countries allied to the West; it has degenerated at points into little more than a knee-jerk and childish reaction against anything that middle America and middle Britain consider valuable or worthwhile.

There are plenty of other absurd examples of the way in which the Left has been hijacked by special-interest groups. One can think of how the trendy poststructuralist thinker Michel Foucault, whose academic work was targeted at unmasking the secret agendas of those with power, welcomed the Islamic Revolution in Iran in 1979. More recently, I was struck at the outrage that greeted Barack Obama's choice of Rick Warren, the megachurch pastor, to pray at his inauguration. I have many questions and concerns about Warren's theology, but I take my hat off to him in terms of the various social causes to which he has committed himself and devoted time and money, including projects to help the poor both in America and abroad. What was interesting was that all his admirable work on behalf of the suffering and the physically destitute counted as nothing to the pundits of the Left in the light of his opposition to gay marriage. So a man who has helped to feed the hungry and clothe the naked is still regarded as a callous, right-wing head case by a group of middle-class commentators and activists, simply because he is opposed to allowing middle-class homosexuals and lesbians to achieve middle-class respectability. It is a strange world where well-fed television hosts, dressed in Armani suits, Vera Wang dresses, and Jimmy Choo shoes, trash a man with an exemplary record on poverty, simply because he cannot support a middle-class lobby group. But such is the hijacking of the Left by those whose agendas are far removed from the old-nineteenth- and early-twentieth-century vision of the universal franchise, decent wages and working conditions, basic health care, and sanitary housing. Call me old-fashioned, but I am not sure that stopping Melissa Etheridge from marrying her partner and enjoying the consequent tax breaks and hospital visiting privileges is in quite the same league of importance as providing clean water to a village in Africa or polio vaccinations for children in Asia, or helping to stop the street violence in Philadelphia. Yet the former cause seems to grip the imagination of the political parties far more than any of the latter.

EVANGELICALS AND THE NEW LEFT

Most of us have come across those evangelicals who, in reaction to the Religious Right, like to parade the fact they vote Democratic in a kind of schoolboyish "Aren't I naughty?" kind of way. It's often an empty gesture, a kind of theological vegetarianism; vegetarians do something that costs them nothing, but my, oh my, does it not make them feel morally superior to the rest of us. So many of the evangelical intelligentsia have bought the concerns of the New Left, with its nebulous and psychologized notions of oppression, which allow for many a "right on" gesture that costs them nothing. Even as I wrote this chapter, the evangelical world threw up an example that shows that, as usual, the trendies of American evangelicalism ape the wider culture, always a day late and a dollar short, and always in a way that makes them look ridiculously sanctimonious and self-important. In February 2010, Dr. Philip Ryken, the pastor of Tenth Presbyterian Church in Philadelphia, accepted the position of Wheaton College's president. Immediately, the blog world erupted with the noise of heartfelt cries about how dreadful it was that the job was being given to a middle-class white male intellectual rather than a representative of a minority (as defined by the middle-class consensus, one presumes). Most of the cries, of course, came as usual from—ahem—middle-class white intellectuals, with quite a few male representatives among them; but not one of those intellectuals was, as far as I know, resigning his own job in order to make way for a minority candidate and to help with the ending of oppression. Thus the self-righteous outrage was as self-contradictory as it was predictable—a typical display of New Left concerns that cost the whiners nothing and were therefore worth nothing. They mewled and they puked, but they did not hold themselves to the same standard to which they wished to hold the Wheaton board and Dr. Ryken. Nor, perish the thought, did they see themselves as candidates to make self-sacrificial examples for others. It is so much easier to lob brickbats at others—and it helps the conscience so much to do it in a righteous cause—than it is actually to make a costly stand oneself. The whole phenomenon was quite simply a sickening display of smugly self-righteous indignation; yet the verdict on Dr. Ryken, the quintessential middle-class white man, is surely just, for a jury of his peers has after all delivered it.

Far from standing as a testimony against the culture and for biblical categories of oppression and liberation, the trendy evangelical Left on display that day clearly enjoys empty, conscience-salving gestures as much as the trendy political Left. After all, it is far easier to sit at a Starbucks Wi-Fi hot spot taking blog swipes at college appointments, or moaning about the mere existence of a few small Protestant denominations that do not ordain women (and whose mere existence seems to "oppress" those who have never even darkened their doors), than to address real matters of oppression, persecution, and tyranny in the world.

CONCLUSION

For someone like me, here lies the heart of the problem of the New Left: once the concerns of the Left shifted from material, empirical issues—hunger, thirst, nakedness, poverty, disease—to psychological categories, the door was opened for everyone to become a victim and for anyone with a lobby group to make his or her issue the Big One for this generation. "Authenticity" and "inauthenticity" are entirely subjective categories, and forms of oppression are thus whatever the oppressed person claims them to be. This is why the media outrage that greets a perceived racist or homophobic comment often far outstrips that which greets scenes of poverty and famine, and it is what leads the likes of Richard Rorty to compare the Holocaust of the Jews in the 1930s and 1940s to the treatment of homosexuals in America and to do so with an apparently straight face. At that point, we are truly in a la-la land with no moral compass, a place that should provoke nothing but ridicule and contempt. This is not to say that bigotry of any kind is at all acceptable or desirable, but to argue that the Left has lost all sense of proportion with regard to what is and is not of most pressing importance. It has become, by and large, the movement of righteous rhetorical pronouncements on total trivia.

As the Left adopted such concerns as gay rights and abortion as touchstone issues, those of us with strong religious convictions on these matters found ourselves essentially alienated from the parties to which our allegiance would naturally be given. The parties of the Right, while representing to an extent, and at least on paper, positions on these matters with which we are comfortable, yet also represent policies in other areas where we find ourselves in fundamental disagreement. If you do not think an untrammeled free market is the answer to society's ills, and if you believe there is such a thing as society and government that, as the democratically elected instrument of that society, has a role to play in health care and helping the poor, where do you turn in a world where the big issues on the Left are gay marriage and a woman's right to choose? Thus I find myself politically homeless, restless, and disenchanted, and I suspect I am not alone.

Now, I need to anticipate the argument of a later chapter here: I believe that on certain issues there is no obviously "Christian" position. I am inclined to include among such issues the wars in Iraq and Afghanistan, the appropriateness of trade unions, rates of direct and indirect taxation, etc. To make any of these things acid tests of Christian orthodoxy is to go well beyond anything the Bible teaches or that the church has felt it necessary to define over the two thousand years of its existence.

Even more, however, I believe that even on those issues where Christians agree on what the end results should be, there is yet room—significant room—for Christians to disagree on how these might be achieved. Thus, for example, it is an unequivocal demand of God's Word that Christians are to love their neighbors. The parable of the good Samaritan, answering the question "Who is my neighbor?" and ending with the imperative "Go and do likewise," would seem to be only the most obvious text to address this matter. Now, if one happens to believe that the untrammeled free market, deregulation, massive defense budgets, and paltry domestic infrastructure spending are not the best ways to address this biblical imperative, where does one turn? Not to the Republican Party, for whom these matters have become virtual mantras. Yet the Democrats seem to be in thrall to precisely the kind of middle-class identity politics of the gay and pro-choice lobbies in which the real oppressed—the poor—are of only marginal concern. Hence, I suspect, the fact that so many of the American working class have—in a move that should seem bizarre—shifted their allegiance to the Republican Party because this party at least makes an attempt to appear to stand for the kind of social values that are of concern to them.

So in this first chapter, I bring nothing for the comfort of those Christians who want to stand with the Old Left on issues such as poverty; we have nowhere to call home. We are despised by those who claim to speak for the oppressed but only seem to speak for those whose notion of oppression is somebody, somewhere, telling them they have to take responsibility for their own irresponsibility or that certain self-indulgent behavior is unacceptable. The progressive intellectuals and the parties of the Left have, by and large, been raptured to a world of identity politics, pampered celebrity endorsements and agendas, and middle-class lobby groups, and we old-school types have been left behind. Let's just hope that the tribulation does not last too long.

The Slipperiness of
Secularization

ONE OF THE MOST striking things about America, at least from the perspective of a British person, is just how explicitly religious much of the politics is. As an outsider, I was well aware of the First Amendment, separating church and state, before I arrived on USA shores. Britain, of course, is very different: the Anglican Church is the established church in England and Wales; the Church of Scotland has the same position "north of the border," as they say. In America, however, it is part of the very foundation of the country that no church and no particular religion enjoys such similar privilege.

Of course, debates still rage over exactly what was the intent of the First Amendment, and scarcely a month goes by without some legal case making the headlines relative to issues such as the placing of copies of the Ten Commandments in a public space.

Many Christians see the exclusion of such explicit religious symbols as a denial of America's heritage; many secular people see the same as a vital part of maintaining freedom and the American way. To the outsider, the passion aroused by the debates is often simply confusing, perhaps a sign that, sometimes, one has to be an insider in a culture truly to understand the emotions generated by some issues.

AMERICA, THE EXCEPTION?

Given the First Amendment, the religious nature of so much political discourse in the States is surprising, but it does fit in general with what has been seen, at least until recently, as part and parcel of American exceptionalism. This is a wide-ranging thesis that basically argues that the way society has developed in America is exceptional in that it does not follow the pattern of social development found elsewhere. Religion is central to this argument: while the development of modern technological societies elsewhere in the world has led to the decline of public, institutional religion, this has not occurred to nearly the same extent in America. The obvious evidence for this is attendance at places of worship, which is very high in the USA but pitifully low in Europe.

In fact, as the years roll by, it looks increasingly as if secular Europe is the exception, and not America. Religion around the world seems to be on the rise, particularly in places such as Africa. Only in Europe, among the old, indigenous populations, does religion seem to be in any kind of terminal decline; elsewhere, the religious future looks really quite rosy. The rise of modern society does not seem, in general, to be quite as opposed to traditional religion as was once supposed.

I want to ask the question, however, whether America was ever that great an exception to secularization, or whether secularization can take various forms, some of which, ironically, look really rather religious at first glance. Could it be that both Britain and America are both fairly secular, but that America expresses her secularity using religious idioms, while Britain expresses hers through the abandonment of such language? And could this create more problems for the American church than she typically likes to assume?

BRITISH CHRISTIANITY: THE DYING OF THE LIGHT

Before I can lay out my thesis on America, however, it is important to spend a few moments outlining the collapse of Christianity in Britain. The nineteenth century in Britain witnessed some spectacular successes for Christianity in terms of missions, urban pastoral care, and the significance of the church in politics, and there was tremendous religious optimism in the air, as the large number of church buildings constructed during this time indicates. Many of these today now stand empty or have been turned to alternative uses, from homes to nightclubs, a fact that is taken by many to indicate a catastrophic collapse in church attendance over the last hundred years. In fact, it is highly unlikely that all of these nineteenth-century churches were ever full; it is probable that many were built merely on the assumption that they would be needed rather than any reality of massive church growth; but even if they were not all full, the very fact they were built indicates the church's optimism, if not triumphalism, coinciding with the height of British imperial power and ambition.

It is also worth noting at this stage the social role of churches and churchmen in key developments during the nineteenth century. The end of the slave trade in the early part of the century was closely connected to the activism of churchmen such as John Newton and the political activity of evangelical MPs including William Wilberforce. The churches were also closely connected with moves to address urban poverty, set up trade unions, and even found the Labour Party as a means of providing advocacy at the highest level for the poor and the working classes. Thanks to the peculiar constitutional history of England, nonconformists (those Protestants who were not Anglicans) had been excluded from Parliament, universities (i.e., Oxford and Cambridge), and the civil service from the mid-seventeenth to the mid-nineteenth centuries; this meant that many of both the captains of industry and the working classes had been "chapel" as opposed to "church." Thus there was a class divide in English Christianity, which meant that a certain social radicalism was associated with nonconformity, perhaps in a manner somewhat analogous to that which exists within African-American Christianity in the USA. Indeed, such was the connection between nonconformist Christianity and political radicalism that the term *Christian socialism* was not—and, indeed, perhaps is not—as strange to the ears of an Englishman as it is to the typical American evangelical.

With the First World War, however, Britain was transformed. The jingoism that surrounded a war of previously unimaginable slaughter was inversely proportional to its rationale. Indeed, while at school I did a special project on the origins of the Great War and, at the end of the course, was barely more capable of explaining the causes than I had been at the start. In retrospect, it appears as the first major crisis in what was to be the century that witnessed the collapse of European imperialism. On the ground at the time, it looked very much like a conflict caused by the upper classes and paid for by the workers.

The collapse of the church in Britain in the years after the Great War is a sorry tale and cannot be reduced to a single cause. The sense of class betrayal induced by the war played a part, as did the sheer magnitude of the horror of the trenches, which, like the Holocaust of the 1940s, raised acute questions regarding the existence of God not just for philosophers but also for ordinary men and women. In addition, the increasing dominance of trade unions and the Labour Party by secular politicians, along with the rise of the welfare state, placed social and political radicalism increasingly in the hands of men and women for whom the church was at best a place of worship, at worst an anachronism.

The Britain in which I grew up in the 1970s and 1980s was very different from that which one would have found a hundred years earlier. Church attendance had declined to pitifully low levels and continues its downward spiral today; and while immigration and the rise of Islam have added a very vocal but still very small Muslim sector to the British population, on the whole Britain, in idiom and actuality, is now a very secular place.

THE USA: SECULARIZATION, RELIGIOUS-STYLE

In the USA, the story is very different, evident in a variety of ways. Church attendance, while varying from state to state, is much higher than in Europe. I remember being at a worship service in Grand Rapids in the mid-1990s and hearing the pastor lament in a sermon that "the tragedy of this town is that only one in two people will be in church this morning." Wow, I thought to myself, that's a tragedy? Back home we'd call that a revival beyond our wildest dreams. In context, of course, the figures no doubt did represent a decline from earlier generations, and it is also easy to become so used to minuscule church attendance that one can become jaded about what is really the tragedy of half the population not worshiping on a Sunday. But my point is that, while Grand Rapids may be exceptional even by American standards, this anecdote still points to the generally much higher church commitment in the USA than in Europe.

Historians and sociologists will no doubt debate the reasons for the difference between America and Europe for years to come. Various factors probably account for the difference: Europe's twentieth century was one of declining world influence, America's of an increase of the same, thus helping to foster pessimism and optimism within the respective cultures; Europe saw horrible slaughter and genocide and significant civilian casualties in a series of major conflicts, while American soil was by and large protected from such terrors, even as she lost large numbers of young men overseas. America also never developed the kind of labor movements found in Europe, had no state church, and contained vast tracts of land where the economy and the lifestyle were rural, agrarian, and thus typically conservative and traditional in culture.

The question I want to ask here, however, is this: Is it actually the case that the American church has maintained the loyalty of large sections of the population by essentially becoming a secular institution? Could it be that secularization might merely have taken a different form in America from that which we find in Europe?

We can start with a soft target: the health, wealth, and happiness teaching of men such as Joel Osteen and Benny Hinn. One listens in vain to their addresses for the kind of talk one finds in Paul's letters to the Corinthians, where he writes of the cross as providing not only a logic to God's saving action in Christ, but also a paradigm for ministry. The suffering that marks Paul's life is essential for his ability to minister to others who suffer, that he might bring them comfort (e.g., 2 Cor. 1). Instead, Osteen and Hinn, in their different ways, point their listeners toward an allegedly happy life, free of pain, want, and distress, which is there for the taking if their advice and spiritual guidance is followed.

Somebody asked me recently whether Osteen and Hinn were big in the UK. My answer was simple: no, not at all, nothing like they are here in the USA. Why is that? came the follow-up, to which I replied: They simply wouldn't work in the UK. because the idiom is all wrong; the British do not respond to religious language in the way many Americans do; thus, we have psychobabble self-help gurus, not prosperity preachers. Of course, both preach the same message: prosperity through realizing your own inner potential; but while the British equivalent is obviously secular, the American version has a veneer of orthodox religiosity.

Prosperity preachers are a soft target, particularly from the perspective of conservative, confessional evangelicals. But the identification of worldly or secular ambitions with the gospel is no monopoly of the positive thinkers and the prosperity Pentecostals. The vision—or at least the sales pitch—of all politicians, Left and Right, is more prosperity, more comfort, better health, etc., etc. We may tut-tut at Osteen as he pushes his message of health, wealth, and happiness, but don't many Christians who claim to be orthodox actually nurture similar ambitions? I will argue in the next chapter that the connection often made between economic prosperity and Christianity by conservative Christians is but a more sophisticated and rhetorically toned-down version of the Osteen gospel. For now, let me ask whether, at a more mundane level, many of us assume that God's favor toward us will be typically demonstrated in the categories of health, wealth, and happiness. How many of us are as guilty of Corinthian-style conceptions of what Christianity should look like as Osteen and company? Maybe the difference is that Osteen is simply more open and honest about it.

SECULARIZATION: SUBTLE AND SPECIOUSLY ORTHODOX

Yet there are other ways that secular values creep in to orthodox churches. This point has been made again and again by David Wells, retired professor of theology at Gordon-Conwell Theological Seminary, starting with *No Place for Truth* (1993) and finishing with *The Courage to Be Protestant* (1998). In this latter book, in many ways a summary of his overall thesis, Wells points toward the way in which the therapeutic concerns of modern America, the substitution of the language of "values" for morals, and the rise of a "me first" individual-rights culture have come to dominate not only the secular American landscape but also that of the evangelical church. In his account, both megachurches and emergent churches represent not so much countercultures but different accommodations to the prevailing culture. The former is the church's equivalent of the big-box store with its careful managerial techniques, its pragmatism, and its market-driven, "stack 'em deep and sell 'em cheap" mentality; while the emergent churches, representing a reaction to such crass consumerism, have actually imbibed the slippery epistemologies and eclecticism of postmodernism, which is itself arguably (and ironically) connected consumerism.

Wells' indictment is damning: what he argues is that many churches are as secular in their ambitions and methods as any straightforwardly secular organization. The difference, we might say, is that the latter are just a whole lot more honest about what they are doing. But while his criticisms are primarily focused on megachurches in the church-growth/Willow Creek tradition and on what we might, for want of a better term, call the evangelical Left, is there a case to be made for saying that secular values also pervade the churches that at least think of themselves as tradition-ally Protestant in the way Wells favors?

I believe so, and in a number of significant ways. For example, take the "rights" culture that is so typical of the wider world in which we live, where litigation and lobby groups seem to proliferate. We can all express dismay at the people who are so inept that they do not realize coffee is hot and, to their great surprise, burn themselves when they spill it, and then proceed to sue the vendor for not telling them about the temperature of the steaming liquid in their cups. We have all no doubt rolled our eyes at the latest innocuous action of some employer that has been deemed offensive—and therefore oppressive—to whatever the minority of the month is. There is a clear silliness going on here; after all, if I took offense and felt oppressed and psychologically damaged every time an American comedian made a joke about British dentistry, I would never have the emotional energy to lift myself out of bed in the morning.

But rights culture is no monopoly of the Left in either politics or the church. The Left may have rights to a completely secular public space, to abortion, and to gay marriage, but the Right too has its litany of rights: to carrying firearms, to cheap gas, to minimal taxation. Now, let me be clear: I am not here drawing specific moral equivalence between any one of the rights and any other; rather, what I am pointing out is the way in which the language of Left and Right is typically couched in that of individual rights, whatever the specific issues might be.

This plays itself out in the church. What is the vow most often breached, even in conservative, confessional churches? It is the vow each member typically takes to submit to the leadership of the church. While the wording varies from church to church, here is that used in my own denomination, the Orthodox Presbyterian Church:

> Do you agree to submit in the Lord to the government of this church and, in case you should be found delinquent in doctrine of life, to heed its discipline?

The assumptions of this vow are clear: Christianity is a corporate phenomenon; it is bigger than me and my own agenda, and it involves disciplined obedience within the church, obedience to which we are bound by vow.

There are those, of course, who argue that church membership is not mentioned in Scripture and is therefore unbiblical. This is not the place to address this objection; suffice it here to say that church membership is the practical expression of clear principles of commitment to each other and respect for an established leadership, which are both stated in the Bible. The real problem, I suspect, with many who argue that church membership is unbiblical is not that their consciences are wounded by the notion, but rather that they want to avoid commitment. They want to treat the church as they treat, say, a supermarket or a cinema: they go along and take what they need without the troublesome issues created by a personal commitment.

That is surely the reason this vow strikes hardest against both the consumer-as-king mentality and the suspicion of authority and power structures that is typical of both the Left and the Right in the secular sphere. It is also the vow that has been most weakened by the thing that lies at the very heart of the American dream—the automobile, the means by which we can conveniently run away from any specific church authority when the fancy takes us.

My point here is that those who are confessional and rock-solid in their doctrinal commitments need to realize that secular values can yet pervade the way they think about church, and the Christians of the political Right can be as guilty of this as anyone— perhaps even more guilty, given the Right's radical individualism, as opposed to the typically more communitarian Left.

A nation with a profound sense of the frontier, of the need for each person to look after himself and not to rely on others, has many strengths, and these things are surely part of the reason for America's tremendous success in the twentieth century. Further, the very structure of American government, which, by and large, seems chaotic to the outsider through all its checks and balances, embodies a deep distrust of power and hierarchy at its very core— hardly surprising, given the fact that its basic shape was hammered out in the heat of a rebellion against a British monarch. But the downside of this is that Americans can be suspicious of anyone in authority, and that spills over into the church; when it does so, it represents not biblical teaching but the incursion of secular individualism. There is an obvious irony to criticizing a Joel Osteen for presenting a secular message in the language of Christianity, or the Left for selling out on moral issues and doing so in the name of Christ, when church discipline in Reformed and Presbyterian circles has all but collapsed in the face of "I'll just treat church as another aspect of the consumer culture" mentality whereby, as soon as my itch isn't scratched, or I am asked for some practical demonstration of commitment, I just jump into my automobile and drive to the next church where I can better preserve my autonomy and anonymity.

THE PATRIOT'S BIBLE AND BEYOND

Another area where a secular mentality impacts the church is the identification of the nation of America with God's special people. Again, I need to be clear what I am not saying here: I am not saying that those Christians who want a place in the public square for the Christian voice are guilty of a secular mind-set; many such people simply want their faith to shape the way they think politically, and that is a perfectly legitimate notion. Nor am I concerned with those Christians who are also strongly patriotic; patriotism, love for one's homeland, is generally a good thing as long as it does not morph into an uncritical nationalism or racism. What concerns me is the so-called extreme wing of the "Christian America"-type movements, where the boundary between church and state, and sometimes even biblical history, becomes rather dangerously blurred. An extreme example is provided by the editors of *The Patriot's Bible*, an edition of God's Word that is sold on the basis of its connection to the founding of the USA. Even if we set aside the problem of connecting the American Revolution to Paul's teaching on civil obedience in Romans 13, the promotional video for the Bible is stunning. A series of images and captions makes the point: Adam and Eve, and George and Martha Washington—first families; Moses and Lincoln—freedom fighters; Jesus and the disciples, and the Continental Congress—founding fathers. In case anyone has missed the point, the video ends with the statement, "Sometimes history does repeat itself." Really? Well, no, in this case it actually doesn't repeat itself. Biblical, salvation history is not repeated or recapitulated in the history of the USA or any other nation, for that matter. To make such a claim is puerile, blasphemous nonsense, as bad as, if not worse than, anything Osteen might say in a sermon; and it represents nothing other than the secularization of the gospel message to an idolatrous degree.[1]

Yet even *The Patriot's Bible* pales in comparison with a painting titled *One Nation Under God*, which portrays Jesus (not a great second commandment move) in the center, holding the U.S. Constitution, surrounded by figures from American history, including the noted deists Thomas Jefferson and Thomas Paine. Now, I am a personal admirer of a number of aspects of Jefferson and Paine, but orthodox Christians they emphatically were not, and to include them pictorially in some nostalgic plea for a Christian nation is historically ignorant, blasphemous, and, quite frankly, risible. It would be fascinating to know what the artist's view of the faith is—

1. The video is available at http://www.americanpatriotsbible.com/video.php. Aaccessed 3/2/2010.

presumably some form of Unitarianism? Patriotism is a civic virtue, and certainly not in itself sinful; but make no mistake, notions of patriotism, so dear to the American Right, can also stand alongside the most secular and heretical visions of Christianity, and can even co-opt such visions as part of their agenda.[2]

The pervasive patriot game also plays out in other ways. The series of books by Tim LaHaye and Jerry Jenkins on the end times, books that have become mainstream best sellers, not only present zany and unbiblical eschatology but also promote racial and ethnic stereotypes. Now, as I said in my chapter on the death of the Left, I have little time for identity politics, and my concern is not that there are racial stereotypes in LaHaye's books; it is more the theological message they convey—if a character is European or, heaven forbid, an Arab, then you know he or she is almost certainly a bad guy (or gal); if he or she is American or Jewish, there is a fair chance that the person is on the right side in the unfolding events. The message is clear: American foreign policy, particularly as regards the nation of Israel, makes it an end-time player on the side of the angels in God's grand historical plan. America is God's agent in saving the world.

The second Iraq War also provided plenty of scope for the notion of America as the nation of God. I remember being at a Bible study when somebody made the comment that it was wonderful that God had raised up George W. Bush for such a time as this. Such comments always create tricky situations at Bible studies: one wants to teach people to think more clearly, but to do so in a manner that does not hurt or belittle them.

---

2. The picture can be viewed at http://mcnaughtonart.com/page/view_search/353. Accessed 3/6/2010.

Thus, in response, I asked who had raised up Saddam Hussein. By the expressions on the faces of the people around the table, it was clear that the penny was starting to drop. World leaders, good and bad, are all raised up by God, just as they are toppled by him as well. And, I asked, when the bombs fell on Baghdad and a Christian family was killed, can we say that God was not on their side at that moment, that, although believers, they were outside the love of God simply by virtue of geographical location and ethnicity? The penny finished its descent. No Christian is outside the love of God, whether dying of cancer, killed in a car crash, or the victim of a bombing raid in times of war. No doubt there were Christians fighting in the Iraqi army as they fought in the U.S. Army, in dutiful obedience to the civil magistrate. This is not to relativize the conflict but to say that the morality of a war cannot be determined simply by the religious makeup of the population or its armies.

The point was simple: the politics of nations and the destiny of God's people, the church, must never be identified. The Bible gives us no basis for doing that. America is, of course, not the first to do this. Augustine at the start of the fifth century wrestled with how to make sense of the sacking of Rome. How could this city, whose name and culture had been so dominant for so long, be brought so low? And England, at the height of her empire, was as guilty as anyone of identifying the English way with God's way. In my office at Westminster I have the gilt-edged cover of an old Bible with the words "The Holy Bible—The Secret of England's Greatness" inscribed on the front. Although there is—symbolically?—no Bible attached to the board anymore, I can probably date the edition to within ten years, because that kind of sentiment is generally characteristic of a nation at the height of its political and military power.

The question to ask about such things—the identification of the Bible with England in the nineteenth century, or American foreign policy in the twenty-first—is "What does this do to the reach of the gospel and the church?" The answer is simple: It creates a dividing line in the church, which is unbiblical. There is no Jew or Gentile in Christ's church; nor should there be any English or American; patriotism is a fine civic virtue and Christians should be good citizens, but it should be checked at the church door as we enter the threshold of Christ's kingdom, not that of Thatcher or Clinton or Bush. If I have to sign up to believe in the manifest destiny of the English-speaking people, or of a particular political project, in order to be a member of Christ's church, or even simply to feel that I belong, then it is arguable that, whoever's church it is, it is no longer the property of Christ but of some more earthly power.

Perhaps, with the rise of China and the problems of the American economy, America is past the zenith of its power and the temptation to identify its way with God's way will decrease, but the general rule remains in place: whatever the temptations may be for the dominant nation at any point in world history to identify its mission with the mission of God, such temptations must be resisted at all costs; God's providential dealings with his people (the church, not any particular nation) are too mysterious to be reducible to simplistic nationalism; and the gospel requires only repentance for sin and faith in Christ, not subscription to specific foreign policies of any particular nation. To demand the latter is to go down the road of the secular mind-set.

THE CELEBRITY SYNDROME

One final aspect of the secular nature of much conservative Christianity is its increasing preoccupation with superstars. This is important, because so often we identify the secular mind-set with content—prosperity doctrine, social gospel, straight-down-the-line antisupernatural liberalism; sometimes, however, the secular mind-set is evident not so much in content but in form, a more slippery and surreptitious thing, and it is in this category that I would place the superstar phenomenon. Confessional superstars might be thoroughly orthodox; they may not even like being superstars; but the people and churches who treat them as such betray the creeping secularism in their own mind-sets.

Paul is clear in his letters to the Corinthians. Corinth was a culture where orators—public speakers—were the rock stars of their day. They prided themselves on their ability to declaim eloquently on any given topic, they attracted disciples and fans, and they carried weight within the wider culture. The problem Paul highlights in the Corinthian church, particularly in his first letter, is that members of the church were using the standards of the secular world in order to judge the quality of their own church leaders. The result was a set of factions or, perhaps even better, fan clubs within the church, focused on great preachers; and Paul, being, according to his own account, not a physically or rhetorically impressive man, was being dismissed as a second-rater. We can perhaps summarize the Corinthian problem by saying that the church had developed an essentially secular mentality: the criteria of the non-Christian world that surrounded them had come to control how they thought about the ministry and its representatives.

Cults of personality are very bad things; the role of the preacher is to point to Christ and, in that context, to be as invisible as possible. The preacher who brings attention to himself would seem to be, by Paul's standards, a failure; more than that, a congregation that focuses on the preacher has failed to understand the power and logic of the cross and has capitulated to a secular mind-set. Yet the conservative church in America is, arguably, driven to a large extent by such cults of personality.

There are a number of pieces of evidence that point toward this. First, there are the parachurch ministries that have sprung up that are focused on the big personality, and frequently named after that personality. Then there is the proliferation of big conferences with big-name speakers. There is nothing intrinsically wrong with such things; but it is clear from even a glance at the Internet or commonplace conversations after church that these things have fostered an ecclesiastical equivalent of stardom where it is not the gospel or even the church that provides the focal point, but Speaker X or Speaker Y.

It is very clear that the Lord has blessed the church of today with some remarkably talented individuals who have been used to do remarkable things. One thinks of Tim Keller in New York, John Piper in Minneapolis, Mark Driscoll in Seattle. The danger is that, in focusing on such men, we create unrealistic expectations. The evidence that the church models developed by these men can be transplanted with success elsewhere is highly equivocal; more likely, their success is rooted in God's using their own remarkable gifts and contexts—the right men in the right place at the right time for something great, if you like. The life of Don Carson's father, outlined so movingly in his *Memoirs of an Ordinary Pastor*, is more likely to be closer to the norm for most churches and pastors than is that of Redeemer in New York.

More importantly, we must recognize the preoccupation with such personalities for what it is: a distraction from the very thing for which these men have themselves worked so hard—a single-minded focus on Jesus Christ. So from whence does the problem come? It comes from imbibing the obsessions of the wider culture with big personalities. The world has Access Hollywood; the church has—well, you insert the name. But the name has to be of someone who is able to build a big church, gain a big name, and offer a sanctified equivalent of the movie-star magic. This is secularization of the church just as surely as *The Patriot's Bible* or the social gospel of Walter Rauschenbusch.

CONCLUSION

Secularization is slippery; it hits us where we least expect it; and there is naught here for comfort of conservative evangelicals. What is needed is continual reformation that takes us back to the standards of God's Word again and again, drives us to repentance, and leads us to put our trust once again in Jesus Christ rather than any set of political policies, or patriotism, or just a nebulous sense that we are better than the rest.

3

Not-So-Fantastic Mr. Fox

BIAS? WHAT BIAS?

News media are, by their very nature, informative and annoying in equal measure. Visiting home recently, I was shocked to see that, in my nearly nine-year absence, the BBC. seems to have been taken over by a bunch of New Labour groupies, intent on competing with each other to see who could be most blind and shortsighted with regard to the shortcomings of the Labour government of Gordon Brown and his merry men. I love the BBC, but "the Beeb," as we call it back in the UK, has both strengths (foreign reporting) and weaknesses (an inability to see Gordon Brown for who and what he is). Of course, this paragraph reeks of my own prejudices; and if you want to know whether, or how far, I speak truly, you need to watch the various British news outlets for yourself.

Mainstream-media bias often tends to be center or left of center. Certainly, in the USA, that appears to be the case with, say, MSNBC and CNN, although, of course, what appears "left" depends on how far one is to the "right." This has led to a certain understandable reaction in Christian quarters against what is often referred to as the liberal media. As someone brought up on the British tradition of pantomime, I have always enjoyed watching and hearing things that I find outrageous and with which I disagree. It can be fun, cathartic, challenging, and just a great opportunity for shouting in frustration at the television screen. More seriously, it can be a reality check on my own assumed biases. While this may not lead me to change them in any fundamental way, it can yet lead me to rethink, sharpen, and reformulate my opinions on key topics. But my great fear is that Christian frustration with the liberal media has led to an overreaction that has generated a culture where alternative opinions are never, or rarely, considered, and where the most inarticulate and insubstantial arguments are swallowed whole. Central to this unfortunate phenomenon is Fox News, the conservative news outlet that is, in many ways, merely the counterpart to the sound-bite purveyors of the Left.

Some weeks after arriving in the USA, I was told by one helpful Christian friend that I needed to make sure I watched Fox News each night because, and I quote, "that's the unbiased news channel." Numerous thoughts sprang to mind at that point, not least the distinction I routinely make as a historian between "objectivity" and "neutrality." I like to argue in class that in the writing of history, no one can be neutral, but historians can be objective. We write narratives from a variety of perspectives; we are all biased to some extent; but these perspectives are publicly testable by established methods of historical verification and falsification. Some historians reject this distinction, but no reputable historian of whom I am aware would argue that it is possible to write "unbiased" history.

Thus encouraged by this friend's counsel and excited that I might be on the verge of discovering that Holy Grail of historical epistemology—an approach to reporting past events that was completely unbiased—I turned on, tuned in, and—ahem—dropped my jaw to the floor. What I witnessed on Fox News was far from unbiased; rather, it was the most unremitting diet of radical conservative political commentary to which I had ever been exposed. Any who criticized US foreign policy were decried as anything from subversive liberals to un-American traitors; Democrats were ridiculed *en masse* as venal and corrupt; Europeans were all gutless socialists; and any dissent from the most robust conservative philosophy was seen as a sign of basic moral failure.

Now, before we go further, I do want to point out that I have no problem with a news service's taking a strong stand on any given issue, or with its pushing a strong political line. After all, as I stated above, I do not believe in the possibility of being unbiased, so I can scarcely criticize someone for having a viewpoint and allowing it to shape that organization's approach to news reporting and commentary. I also have no problem with outrageous overstatement to make a point, no doubt being guilty of it myself on various occasions. The problem is neither of these things; rather, it is the failure to notice that these two things are actually happening. To refer to Fox News as "the unbiased one" is to make the mistake of thinking that all one gets on Fox are "the facts" while everyone else—the BBC World Service, MSNBC, CNN, etc., etc.—gives some kind of spin.

SERMONS FOR THE FAITHFUL

The strange thing is that American conservative Christians can be as partisan about their news channels as they are about their political parties, in large part because of the partisan alignment of those channels. I recently had dinner with a minister friend who told me how he had received comments from concerned church members when he had mentioned seeing some news story on MSNBC. And I have been rebuked myself on more than one occasion for citing the Huffington Post, a well-known liberal blog, in public comments, even though, as far as I can remember, the citations referred to stories that were not remotely political. The very act of citing the Huffington Post—the mere hint that it might contain something worth reading—was enough to provoke a reaction, as if the presence of a statement such as "There has been an earthquake in Haiti" was rendered less true, or inherently subversive, by the fact that somebody left of center had written it.

As an example of Fox punditry, take Glenn Beck, for instance. He is rapidly becoming the most popular conservative pundit in America, and a Fox stalwart. Here is a fairly typical quotation:

> Now, we've got a choice to make: Do we choose the [sic] fundamentally transform America to a Marxist, spread the wealth, cradle to grave nanny state? Where no one gets a boo-boo? And, as we have seen in country after country, is only sustainable through the barrel of a gun? Or do we come to our senses and realize that spending and taxing kills business? And stop with the pensions that literally pay out 30 times what we put into them![1]

1. http://www.foxnews.com/story/0,2933,586983,00.html. Accessed 2/22/2010.

Numerous thoughts come to mind. First, it is hard to take seriously a man who identifies Marxism with the welfare state. Marxism is actually a philosophy of history and economic organization that sees class struggle and the movement of capital as the inevitable dynamo driving history along; the welfare state is no more distinctively the preserve of Marxism than philosophical ignorance is distinctively the preserve of talk-show hosts. Second, the claim that a welfare state is designed to stop anyone from getting a "boo-boo" is nonsense. As I searched high and low on Mr. Beck's Web site, I could find no data to support his claim that that was indeed the intention in any of the modern developed democratic economies with a welfare state (and as far as universal health care provision goes, that's all of them, bar the USA). Third, where are these countries where the welfare state is enforced "only. . . through the barrel of a gun"? As I said, we are talking here about every democratic industrialized country other than the USA, not places such as North Korea and Myanmar.

For myself, I hardly ever saw a gun while growing up in the UK, and then only shotguns in the hands of farmers scaring crows. And when I visited the Continent, I saw them only in the holsters of the occasional policeman. There are probably more government-bought bullets fired in law enforcement on the streets of Philadelphia each year than in the entire UK, and that surely raises the question of which countries we are talking about that keep order by the barrel of a gun. Beck's argument (and I use the word in its very loosest sense) is drivel—a concatenation of portentous-but-meaningless rhetoric. It reveals no real knowledge of the issues involved, and is apparently designed merely to confirm prejudices and stir up passions among those who are presumably already on board with the somewhat scary Beckian view of the world where "they" are apparently always out there, trying their best to "get us." Certainly, those who disagree with him will find nothing here—evidence, logic, careful use of clearly defined technical terms—to cause them to change their minds. Besides, one suspects that the request for such evidence might well be greeted as just another bleeding-heart liberal attempt to subvert the American way, as defined by Mr. Beck. Like Rush Limbaugh, Mr. Beck is undoubtedly amusing. I like to think of him as a comedy turn in the Monty Python D. P. Gumby "flower arranger" mold, but we should never confuse a loudmouth, a microphone, and a talent for outrage with real political discussion.

Another of the popular Fox pundits is Bill O'Reilly, whose show, *The O'Reilly Factor*, claims to be the number-one cable news talk show. O'Reilly certainly is a more civil character than Beck, lacking the latter's loutish approach and sheer decibel level, but his material, too, is often little more than a collection of populist conservative clichés. Take the following comment on socialism:

> A recent Gallup poll is simply incredible. Thirty-six percent of Americans have a positive image of socialism, including 53 percent of Democrats. Just 17 percent of Republicans think socialism is good.
>
> Now, socialism is the exact opposite of capitalism, which is our system in America. A socialist believes the government has a right to control and/or seize private property and regulate the distribution of goods and services.

That means the government has all the power. You have none. Can you say Fidel Castro? And 53 percent of Democrats think that's a positive thing? It's hard to believe.[2]

Now, while Hugo Chavez might take some comfort from the fact that even 17 percent of Republicans seem to like socialism, there are all sorts of problems here. *Socialism*, as with most if not all terms ending in *-ism*, is a word that covers a broad spectrum of concepts. It is thus misleading to claim that it is "the exact opposite of *capitalism*, which is our system in America." In fact, capitalism (another of those pesky *-ism* terms) is also a term with a broad range of meanings, at least when it comes down to what it looks like in practice. Arguing such matters at a purely abstract, undefined level is unhelpful. Strictly speaking, for example, a Mafia protection racket and your friendly neighborhood drug dealer are both examples of capitalism. I doubt that Mr. O'Reilly would want me to base my definition of *capitalism* on those two examples, however; nor would it be legitimate to do so and then claim that capitalism is, therefore, "the exact opposite" of law enforcement.

I am not a socialist and never have been, but my grandparents were, and for the record, neither of them believed that the government had the right to control or seize private property in the kind of unconditional way implied by O'Reilly. His argument is logically fallacious, and can be expressed as follows: Fidel Castro is a socialist; Fidel Castro believes the government has the right to control and seize private property; therefore socialism is the view that the government has the right to control and seize private property. By similar logic, Denny the Dealer is a capitalist; Denny

2. http://www.foxnews.com/story/0,2933,585592,00.html. Accessed 2/22/2010.

the Dealer believes he has the right to sell illegal drugs to whomever he chooses; therefore capitalism is the view that the individual has the right to sell illegal drugs to anybody and everybody, regardless of the law of the land. The argument is nonsense, yet O'Reilly is perhaps the most popular pundit on television, and certainly influential in conservative Christian circles. It is embarrassing to see that such poorly argued material seems to carry so much weight and proves to be so influential with so many.

In actual fact, the difference between democratic capitalism and democratic socialism is that of a sliding scale—a debate about the extent of state power. Any nation with armed forces or a system of roadways has, at some point, almost certainly had a government that has issued a compulsory purchase order on a piece of previously private property. I presume even Messrs. Beck and O'Reilly occasionally use roads built under such circumstances to get to their offices and studios. Generally speaking, even in the USA the basic elements of national defense are not sold off to the highest bidder, despite the recent advent of "private security firms" (previously known as mercenary outfits); rather, they are the preserve of the government. To extend government competence to health care, for example, is not to become Castro's Cuba. Rather, it is simply an extension of what is already conceded in principle: pure private enterprise is not adequate for meeting all of society's needs. Such an extension may or may not be desirable, but it is not a debate between heroes of freedom and aspiring tin-pot Stalins. And it is not at all clear where capitalism ends and socialism begins, given the mixed nature of all Western economies. It is only at the extreme of Communism that one finds socialism of the peculiar variety that Mr. O'Reilly seeks to make normative.

The simplistic nature of O'Reilly's thinking is highlighted even more when he continues in a subsequent paragraph to mention China, as if that country, too, were an example of socialism as he describes it. Not so. Even a conservative thinker like Francis Fukuyama, while acknowledging the complexity of defining exactly what China's economy does represent, opts for the term *authoritarian capitalism* rather than *socialism*.[3] If nothing else, the Chinese phenomenon indicates that the old polarities of capitalism and socialism, so crucial to the simple universe inhabited by O'Reilly and company, are no longer adequate to describe the world—if indeed they ever were.

OK, so Beck and O'Reilly are not the most knowledgeable or logical conservative commentators; but what is really worrying is that they and their colleagues at Fox seem to set many of the basic trajectories and provide much of the unquestioned data for conservative Christians in their thinking about the world (don't forget, they work for the unbiased news channel). And given their slippery logic, extensive use of terms of which they seem to have little grasp, sweeping statements about other nations that are (as with those about Britain) frequently incomprehensible to those from such countries, and somewhat (!!) black-and-white Manichaean view of the universe, this should be a cause for concern, especially among Christians, who should know that the world is just a whole lot more complicated than a goody-baddy sound-bite scenario will allow, and who should also have a high regard and concern for the truth and for fair speaking. Yet, while MSNBC (or "PMSNBC," as Rush Limbaugh sometimes refers to it) is dismissed variously as "liberal" or even "Marxist," Fox enjoys this peculiar status as the

3. "Is the Age of Democracy Over?" *The Spectator*, February 13, 2010.

conservative evangelicals' station of choice. So this begs the question: How amenable to Christian thinking is this hallowed source of all world knowledge?

A TASTE OF THEIR OWN CONSPIRACY THEORY

Given that much of what Beck, O'Reilly, and company peddle on Fox is a form of conspiracy theory—that "they" (the elites, the liberals, the Democrats, the people from MSNBC, the feminists, the Europeans, the Arabs, etc.) are out to destroy the American way of life (at least as Beck and O'Reilly define it)—I would beg the reader's indulgence at this point to allow me to do a little bit of conspiracy theorizing myself. Take the owner of the network, media mogul Rupert Murdoch, a world player if ever there was one. Now, just because a man owns a company does not mean that he shapes everything that happens in it, and this is surely the case with a business as large and as complicated as Mr. Murdoch's media empire. Yet Murdoch has for decades had a reputation as a man who plays a very proactive role in editorial policy for his various outlets—print and televisual. Tony Blair needed to court him to ensure that the British tabloid *The Sun* was on board for the 1997 election, since it seemed that in 1992 *The Sun* had influenced its predominantly working-class readership in such a way that the unpopular Major government managed to hold power in what was a most unexpected victory. The headline in that organ then had been the now-legendary "It's *The Sun* wot won it!," and Blair wanted no repeat of the disaster. If the attention paid to him by politicians, British and American, at election time is any accurate measure, then Murdoch is undoubtedly able to guide editorial policy in most significant ways.

Yet who is Murdoch? For one thing, as I noted in the introduction, he is one of the men responsible for turning me from a young Conservative to (in the British political-party sense) one who now votes Liberal Democrat (although I have never joined the LDP). While he and editors of his organs, such as Andrew Neil of *The Times*, had spent the 1980s standing shoulder to shoulder with Mrs. Thatcher in opposition to Soviet totalitarianism, in the 1990s he seemed to undergo a significant shift when the possibility of fertile new markets in China opened up. That is when he blocked publication of Chris Patten's memoirs of his time as the last governor of Hong Kong, because they might have upset his business dealings. Freedom, it seems, was important only so long as it did not do damage to profit margins.

In his private life, Murdoch is scarcely a paragon of Christian virtue. Now, let me be clear: I see no necessary connection between a businessman's private life and the products he hawks, but when he sells opinions through his media outlets and is well known as a man who takes a proactive interest in the views that are thus propagated, it is at least worth asking about personal moral integrity. Murdoch has been married three times and divorced twice—the second time in a very acrimonious manner. Indeed, the second divorce was followed within weeks by marriage to his third wife. Bottom line: Murdoch himself does not embody the kind of family values that are so near and dear to many conservative Christians. Having said that, as noted in an earlier chapter, while the Christian Right is intolerant of any personal peccadillo on the part of liberals, it is often very forgiving of the private failings of its heroes, as in the case of Rush Limbaugh, with his various marriages and his well-publicized drug addiction.

Beyond his private life, however, Murdoch's media empire is rather selective in its promotion of conservative values—at least as understood by the Christian world. We have already noted the China connection, but democracy is not the only negotiable in Murdoch's world when it comes to money. For example, take *The Sun*—Britain's most popular daily paper, and a tabloid known for setting the bar as low as it gets when it comes to journalism, with its often hilarious but scarcely nuanced front-page headlines, such as "Stick It Up Your Junta!" (from 1982, when Mrs. Thatcher rejected a peace proposal from Argentina during the Falklands conflict), "Freddie Starr Ate My Hamster" (from 1986, and actually a completely fabricated story, much to the relief of the hamster involved), and "Bonkers Bruno Locked Up" (from 2003, a particularly sensitive front-page reference to the hospitalization of former boxer Frank Bruno after he had a nervous breakdown). Most famous of all, however, is *The Sun*'s contribution to nude modeling. Page 3 of the Murdoch-owned British tabloid is famous in Britain for providing the world with a daily diet of beautiful, topless women. Indeed, prior to the advent of the World Wide Web, it is possible that Murdoch was responsible for putting more soft pornography into more houses than anybody else in history. By the standards of the Internet, this is no doubt very low on the scale of sleaze, and these days such pictures are mild compared even with what can be seen in films cleared for teenage viewing, but I wonder how many Christian fathers out there would appreciate opening their morning newspaper and seeing their own daughters, in topless glory, smiling at them from page 3? Probably not too many, yet this is all part of the wider Murdoch empire and of the philosophy that underpins his operation, a philosophy that, the more you look at it, seems pinned less to a particular moral stance than to marketing what product can be sold in which context.

There are, however, even more subtle ways in which Fox in particular undercuts the kind of values that conservative Christians hold dear. Take the popular cartoon *The Simpsons* as an example. Nobody would argue that the Simpson family represents the kind of ideal to which Christian parents aspire, although some of us perhaps fear that our own families often feel closer to what Homer and company embody than we would like them to be. *The Simpsons* is indeed one of Fox's great success stories, and while I do not watch it now, I did catch a few episodes in years past and found it at times to be painfully funny in the way that it did indeed capture something of the nature of living in middle America. We can all, I suspect, recognize others and, in moments of lucidity, even ourselves in some of the characters that the series depicts. How many of us, for example, can watch the "Christian" character Ned Flanders and not see some of the more cringe-making aspects of our own church experience laid bare?

Nevertheless, when we examine the underlying values being projected, what do we have? Children who defy parents (and, quite frankly, parents whose venality and foolishness often makes the children's defiance seem quite an appropriate response in context), Christianity pilloried and presented as a religion of half-witted idiots and sleazy clerics, and all manner of cynical shenanigans condoned and promoted. Of course, the immediate response will be that *The Simpsons* is just a cartoon, and anyone watching can tell the difference between that and reality. Fair enough, although I know of quite a few who pride themselves on being in the vanguard of postmodern evangelicalism who will yet point to Ned Flanders as one reason for breaking the evangelical mold, apparently assuming that he, at least, is merely a mirror of an unpleasant reality that we need to slough off at the earliest opportunity. Yet in a world where the mere mention in Christian circles of the Huffington Post or *The Rachel Maddow Show* (where opinions are worn on the sleeve and open for debate) can provoke cries of horror from the Christian Right, it is surprising that nobody has forged any connection between Fox News and the subtle subversion of *The Simpsons*. They are both part of the same empire, after all, and putting money into the same pockets; maybe, just maybe, they are all part of the same marketing philosophy.

But I am less concerned with the content of *The Simpsons* than with the timing; on the East Coast of the USA, the series is on at 6:00 each evening—typically the sort of time when traditional, conservative types like to think we should all be sitting around the dining table, talking to our children and cementing family relationships. That is, in fact, generally what the Trueman family does at this time, but the activity is scarcely encouraged by Fox's scheduling one of the most popular, long-running, and subversive cartoon series of all time at this very hour. Not exactly promoting the American way, in either its content or its chronological placement, is it? Surely if there is one thing that has done more damage to traditional family dynamics, it has been the advent of the television, and here is a channel exploiting that for all it is worth.

All in all, with soft porn, suppression of free speech, and *The Simpsons*, that's quite a tally for Rupert Murdoch. But let us not forget that this purveyor of topless titillation and underminer of traditional family values is also the copyright holder, through HarperCollins, of the New International Version of the Bible and, as owner of Fox News, the proprietor of the one "unbiased" news channel in the USA.

Strange to tell, not one of the Fox fans I have ever talked to has ever made this connection. The various channels under the Fox logo seem to enjoy the full confidence of many conservatives because of the political line trotted out by the likes of Glenn Beck, Bill O'Reilly, and company about defending the American way and watching out for how the dreaded government (elected, by the way, by the American people) is subverting young people and traditional values—all at the same time those young people and their families are being subverted by the very media empire that presents itself as the last best hope of the traditionalists. Of course, no family *has* to watch *The Simpsons* at 6 o'clock, just as nobody *has* to vote for a liberal candidate at an election or *has* to believe a news report from Rachel Maddow. But what is good for the goose is surely good for the gander, and if Ms. Maddow is seen as a dangerous sign of the times at MSNBC, should we not apply the same measure to the even more subtle and thus potentially more sneakily subversive presences on Fox?

The bottom line is that Fox's political posturing as the brave advocate for and defender of conservative values is just that—a piece of posturing. It is simply one part of an empire that also promotes values and practices that undermine precisely such values, whether it be the soft pornography and juvenile captions of page 3 or the timing and plotlines of *The Simpsons*. Murdoch wants to make money, and in time-honored fashion, he finds out what we like, and how we like it, and he lets us have it just that way.

LET'S USE OUR GOD-GIVEN CRITICAL FACULTIES

The obvious response to all I have written about Fox so far is this: Well, the other channels and outlets are just as bad; they have their biases; their proprietors have their weaknesses and their agendas; and they project views of the world that are selective and involve generous dollops of spin. Well, yes, they do; but my first major point in this chapter was precisely that—all news channels have their biases and their agendas, all are shaped by those who pull the financial strings, and Fox is no exception. So no one should ever spout the "Fox is the unbiased news channel" nonsense, especially Christians, who, with their understanding of the malignant and complex impact of sin on human psychology, should understand the need for a certain skepticism regarding all such media outlets. Fox is not unbiased, never has been unbiased, and frankly never can be unbiased, any more than any other outlet. Yes, it is true that liberal pundit Keith Olbermann is about as nuanced and sophisticated in his political analysis as Glenn Beck and Bill O'Reilly; so, from the perspective of serious political discussion, I say a plague on all their houses.

When it comes to listening to the news, Christians should be eclectic in their approach and not depend merely on those pundits who simply confirm their view of the world while self-evidently using terminology, logic, and standard rules of evidence and argumentation in sloppy, tendentious, and sometimes frankly dishonest ways, such as Mr. Beck and his "welfare means totalitarianism" claims. There is a sense in which we are dependent for our view of the wider world on those media that give us access to that world, so surely it is incumbent on us to make sure that we expose ourselves to a variety of viewpoints on the great issues of the day.

Of course, this is where we find what can only be described as a strange contradiction within the psyche of many conservative Christians. On the one hand, there seems to be a fear that merely reading the Huffington Post or watching *The Rachel Maddow Show* will turn people into rabid, pro-choice Communists; on the other hand, there seems to be no fear whatsoever that conservative media will have the same effect at those points where they deviate from positions consistent with Christianity. Thus there is no fear that watching Glenn Beck will destroy someone's ability to use terms with precision or to treat an alternative perspective with respect, and no one seems concerned that Bill O'Reilly's frequent leaps of logic will leave his audience incapable of constructing a decent syllogism.

In addition, what about all those subliminal signals that are scarcely compatible with Christianity? Fox is a commercial channel, and its programs are punctuated with a large number of advertisements for all manner of things, most of which send the clear signal that the essence of life is the purchase of particular commodities. If you think watching Maddow will turn viewers into lesbians, then you should also believe that commercial television will turn us all into greedy materialists who look no further than our next purchase to find our existential significance.

Either human beings are critical creatures, provided with brains that allow them to think for themselves, or they are mere sponge-like receptors who believe whatever they are told by a third party.

Biblically speaking, it would seem that the former is the case. Luke, for example, constructed his history by talking with eyewitnesses, and we can presume he used only those sources that he found reliable while discounting the rest. When the Bereans heard the gospel, they searched the Scriptures to see whether the things they heard were so. Critical faculties were engaged in both instances.

When Christianity was starting to penetrate the Roman Empire in the second century, there were a number of thinkers, called by scholars the Greek Apologists, who took it on themselves to argue the case for Christianity in the public square. One of their most powerful arguments was that Christians, far from subverting public order (and that, of course, was, at that time, a profoundly un-Christian public order), actually made the very best citizens in terms of hard work, loyalty, and civil obedience. Later, Calvin made essentially the same point in the prefatory letter to his *Institutes of the Christian Religion*. Today, our obligation is no different: we are called to be good citizens in this world, and in a democratic society, that involves having as many well-thought-out and informed opinions on the things that really matter as time allows. It is incumbent on us not to surround ourselves with things that confirm our prejudices but to seek to listen to a variety of viewpoints. The listening is not an end in itself, as so many postmodern conversationalists would have it; the purpose is to become more informed and to have better-grounded and better-argued opinions. But that can happen only when watching the news becomes more than just having our gut convictions continually confirmed.

Thus my basic argument in this chapter is not that people should switch their brand loyalty from Fox to MSNBC or from Glenn Beck to Keith Olbermann. Although the penchant of conservative Christians for a media empire that may spout radical conservative politics but that also engages in activities that run directly counter to all they hold dear is bizarre, it is in this regard only the same as any other channel. The game for media barons is not to communicate the truth; it is to make money, and we should acknowledge that from the start. My point is not that Christians abandon one biased news channel for another; rather, it is that Christians above all people should take seriously their responsibilities as citizens and make every effort to find out as much as they can about the issues that matter. Watch Beck, listen to Limbaugh, or watch Olbermann if you must; but do not mistake these men for serious and thoughtful commentators on the world; rather, they are satirical comedy turns—a bit of fun and nonsense. Watch serious news programs, too, from a variety of channels to make as sure as humanly possible that you are seeing the issues in all their complexity. Better still, buy a decent, thoughtful magazine or newspaper that has the potential of dealing with issues in more than thirty-second sound bites and video clips. Society needs Christians who are better informed and more articulate than the likes of Glenn Beck, Keith Olbermann, or Bill O'Reilly. Let us be Greek apologists once more, and show the civil powers that we can be the best and most informed and thoughtful citizens there are, not those whose stock-in-trade are clichés, slander, and lunatic conspiracy theories.

4

LIVING LIFE TO THE MAX

MAX WEBER: MAKING CAPITALISM BORING

When it comes to politics, the conservative Christian world has produced some strange alliances. The alliance of many good Christian people and Rupert Murdoch's Fox Channel is one of them, operating at the level of popular TV choices. A stranger alliance, and one that has a bit more intellectual ballast, is that between conservative Christians and an influential German thinker, and it is to this that I now turn.

Max Weber (1864–1920) is generally considered, along with Karl Marx and Emile Durkheim, as one of the founders of modern social science. His key text, and the only book that he published in his lifetime, is *The Protestant Ethic and the Spirit of Capitalism.* In this work, he attempted to offer an alternative account of the rise of capitalism to that which Marxism provided. Marxism dealt with capitalism in strictly materialist terms, seeing it as a phase in the ongoing economic struggle between the classes.

Weber, however, argued that the rise of capitalism was more than purely material in ultimate origin. Instead, he saw certain affinities between Protestantism, or at least certain types of Protestantism, and those values and patterns of behavior that were important for facilitating the rise of capitalist life and practice.

To elaborate, Weber saw the Protestant notion of calling—the idea that all tasks, when done to the glory of God, could be sacred—as revolutionary, as indeed it was. In one fell swoop, Luther and his colleagues had abolished the sacred/secular division and the hierarchy that was so central to the medieval way of doing things; yet Weber regarded Luther's approach as still conservative. After all, the Reformer's emphasis on accepting one's calling was, in effect, an argument for the status quo in terms of social position.

For Weber, the real affinity between Protestantism and the capitalist ethic was to be found in the theological tradition of Calvinism. With its accent on predestination, Calvinism created a problem with assurance of God's love—ironic, considering the pivotal role that assurance played in the inception of the Reformation. This in turn led to introspection, the rationalization of life (via the Puritan habit of keeping a diary), and the notion that profit generated by hard work was a sign of election and of God's favor. In time, of course, Weber saw the capitalist ethic as taking on a life of its own and sloughing off the Protestantism that had given it birth; but the initial relationship was, he argued, vital to the shape of capitalism and the speed at which it developed.

Weber's thesis contains numerous problems. First, there is his presentation of Protestantism: the idea that Calvinism generated the kind of individual angst and insecurity for which he argued is a highly debatable proposition, and one that has been subjected to searching theological criticism over the years.

Second, there is an internal difficulty regarding the logic of the argument. Weber seems to assume something—the importance of Protestantism for the phenomena he observes—that he then seeks to prove. In other words, there is a circularity to the argument. The weakness of this can be seen when one throws into the mix other possibilities for the success of capitalism. For example, was it the *Protestantism* of these Protestants that fueled the ethics and behavior that drive capitalism—hard work, resourcefulness, thrift—or was it something else? Perhaps it was not their religion in itself that was significant in this regard but rather the social marginality that their religion involved. Take, for example, the Jews, who have over the years produced some of the most astute representatives of the capitalist community. Is it Protestantism that drives them? Obviously not. Is it some nebulous Judeo-Christian worldview? Possibly, although I have a Jewish friend who objects to that term on the ground that it is generally used by Christians as longhand for *Christian worldview*. More likely, I suspect, it is their marginality—the fact that for large periods of their history in Europe, there was little they could do in terms of establishment positions (civil service, universities, government, etc.), and so all that was left were pursuits such as moneylending, banking, trade, etc.

Certainly, when looking at nineteenth-century Britain, undoubtedly the powerhouse of the Industrial Revolution, one finds nonconformists such as Quakers playing significant roles in the rising industries, and it is not immediately obvious that the tenets of their religion are the primary reason for this. Quakers in particular were scarcely likely to suffer from any alleged Calvinist pathologies. It is at least arguable that the fact that nonconformists had been excluded from the establishment since the seventeenth century meant they had few options for betterment other than trade, industry, etc.

A third problem with Weber is that his account cannot provide a rationale for the rise of the Asiatic economies such as Japan, Korea, and later China, where there is no link to Protestantism. This is arguably not fatal to Weber's thesis in the way that the first point could well be; Weber merely tried to explain why capitalism rose the way it did in western Europe. His is not a deterministic model and so may not apply elsewhere. This point is, however, significant for Christians who like to make a necessary connection between Protestantism and successful capitalism, as we will note below.

A fourth problem with Weber's thesis is that, frankly, he makes capitalism seem rather boring and prosaic—a tedious and gray world of hard work and accumulation. Ironically, Marx was much better on the spirit of capitalism at this point than Weber. Marx understood that capitalism was an exciting, creative, and powerful force that had the ability to reshape any and all realities; and certainly, Marx's description of capitalism is much closer to the reality we know today than that we find in the pages of Weber. In a world of easy credit and high living standards, capitalism is an exciting, attractively designed iPad, not a dusty ledger of debits and credits. There is an excitement, a creativity, a desire to own beautiful things and to enjoy new experiences—whether fine wines or pleasure cruises—that drives the capitalist ethic; and this pleasure in acquisition and accumulation, this desire to have more and to be better, has surely always been there.

ABSOLUTIZING THE MOMENT

Despite the problems with Weber's thesis, it has proved somewhat attractive to American Christians keen to see a close relationship between their theology and a central tenet of the American way—the capitalist free market. The connection is useful: if there is a link between Christian truth and capitalist prosperity, then capitalism itself becomes the God-given way in which society should be organized; and it presumably accounts for the fact that, in the USA, a term such as *socialism* is so often seen as antithetical to Christianity, in a way that would have been historically unthinkable in a place such as Great Britain, where Christians played a key role in the early history of both the Labour Party and the trade-union movement. Indeed, while writing this book I had the privilege of spending a day addressing evangelical pastors in Wales, men who labor in poor, former mining areas. They were incredulous that any evangelical Christian would ever vote for a right-of-center capitalist party; such is the contextual nature of the relationship of theology and politics. Yet in the American context, given the connection between capitalism and the American way, the relationship routinely drawn between Christianity and capitalism would also seem to argue for seeing America's social organization as superior to that of other countries and as specifically blessed by God.

There are a number of problems here. The first, and perhaps the most important, is to realize that a temptation to identify the way things are done in the here and now with the way they should always be done is often unseen but all-pervasive. The nineteenth century produced a number of influential thinkers who saw history as a process, not simply a static state of affairs. On the scientific level, there was Charles Darwin, with his arguments regarding evolution; on the ecclesiastical front, there was John Henry Newman, whose study of the development of doctrine in the early church led him to ask deep questions about the nature of authority and drove him to leave the Church of England and become a Roman Catholic; and on the historical and philosophical front, there was G. W. F. Hegel, and his various intellectual offspring, most notably Karl Marx, who saw the historical process as leading inexorably toward an end point, where all tensions (whether spiritual, as in Hegel, or material, as in Marx) would be resolved.

What all these models had in common was a belief in progress, and that things were moving ever closer to what one might regard as the ideal state of affairs, even if that state would never be perfectly achieved. The same kind of mentality underlies the industrial and scientific mind-set, where the move to great prosperity, efficiency, and more accurate grasp and mastery of reality was seen as part of the task in hand and the necessary result of applying right thinking and effort.

Now, it would be a stretch—a real stretch—to say that America was so profoundly influenced by Hegel that it had come to identify itself with the end of history. But while many Americans may not be self-conscious Hegelians, there is no doubt that the idea that America—in terms of its values, institutions, and general way of doing things—represents the best there is, and the future of humanity, is deeply ingrained in American culture. This is not surprising: it is the typical trait of dominant political powers. Rome was the norm in the first few centuries A.D., and England in the late nineteenth century provides many now-comical examples of what such a culture can produce, with famous sayings to the effect that being born an Englishman was to have won first prize in the lottery of life, and how most people of other nationalities, if asked, would declare that they would rather have been born as Englishmen. America's dominance of the post-World War II West, and its perceived victory in the Cold War, seemed only to reinforce the frontier mentality that the future was there to be conquered, and conquered by the American way.

At the start of the twenty-first century, however, the vision of an American future looks decidedly questionable. The global triumph of its amazing brand of democratic capitalism seems far less certain than it did in 1989. Resurgent Islamic fundamentalism, renewed and violent ethnic conflict around the globe, and, above all, the rise to financial dominance of China call into question all manner of old certainties.

We will talk about China below. The point I am making here is not a political or ideological one; rather, it is simply this: we have no basis for absolutizing the social organization and the attendant institutions, practices, and values of our passing present than anybody in ages past. Feudalism seemed like the wave of the future when it was at its zenith, yet it has passed away, at least in the West. European imperialism seemed set to dominate the world forever and a day at the end of the nineteenth century, but along came two world wars that put an end to that notion. We do well to be aware that we must never assume the way things are done now represents the ideal end of some historical process that is simply getting better and better. That is a pagan idea that also involves a basic idolatry of ourselves and our mores.

To put it bluntly: the fact that American democratic capitalism seems to be the best system for social organization so far devised does not mean that it represents "reality" in a way that has never been done before, nor that it enjoys some status as the end term of economic history and that there will be no further developments beyond its slow and inevitable spread across the face of the globe. What I am not saying here is that it is a bad system; I am simply saying that we should not absolutize it as if it represented the end of history.

The second point about capitalism and the free market is that conservative Christians who seek to minimize the role of the state need to understand that the talk about "the morality of the markets," so popular with free-market philosophers, is highly misleading. The market has only one basic principle: profit; all else is derivative of, and connected to, this one basic point. To listen to some Christians talk, one would think that evil is essentially the preserve of Washington, and that CEOs of private companies have nothing but our interests at heart; or, at least, are forced into dealing fairly with us because they cannot buck the forces of the market. Thus government health care is bad because it will be rationed by bureaucrats; private health care is good because rationing does not exist. Of course, this argument assumes that all insurance companies have unlimited capital at their disposal and employees who would never, ever deny a claim for vital treatment. Thus private insurance companies mean no health care rationing by anonymous bureaucrats. You may laugh, but I have heard arguments that presuppose these latter two statements seriously proposed by Christians discussing this topic.

The genius of Margaret Thatcher and Ronald Reagan was their ability to bind together traditional values (as understood in their two countries) and free-market economics. This allowed for the building of electoral bases across typical class divisions, because the working classes are often more socially conservative than the middle class. Yet what has become clear since the 1980s is that such a combination is remarkably volatile, and arguments based on efficiency, wealth creation, and profit are a dangerous two-edged sword for the conservative Right. One thinks of the recent brouhaha surrounding the vote in California to ban gay marriage—seen as a victory for the conservatives. However, it has been argued since that such a move is highly damaging to an already dire local economy, driving away all the money that might come from the pink dollars of gay tourism. Those who live by the ethic of wealth creation may well find their world dying by the ethic of wealth creation.

For a free marketer, the system is designed to promote maximum efficiency: wages find their appropriate level, supply meets demand, hard work is rewarded, individual power is enhanced, government is limited. Thus runs the theory. Of course, we are self-interested, but the idea is that your self-interest and mine will, if not cancel each other out, at least affect each other and limit the damage that can be done. Inequality will persist, but as long as there is the possibility of social mobility and thus motivation for hard work, this is not a particular problem. Whether this is the case, however, and the market operates this smoothly is now open to question on a variety of fronts, particularly in light of the financial collapse of late 2008. More to the point, should capitalism enjoy the kind of adulation it does in many conservative evangelical quarters?

THERE IS NO ALTERNATIVE, BUT . . .

Several points need to be made here. For a start, I have no doubt that, in the current situation, capitalism of some form is the best means of wealth creation. There is, quite simply, no alternative out there: old-style socialism failed to deliver; the New Left is more preoccupied with the psychology of identity politics than making constructive economic proposals; and by and large, that which distinguishes parties of Right and Left in the developed world is not the affirmation or rejection of capitalism but debates about tax rates, the scope of the public sector, etc.

Having said this, however, we need to be aware of assuming that capitalism is the be-all and end-all of history. Just because there is no alternative at the moment does not mean that democratic capitalism is the end term of social and economic organization. There was no alternative to feudalism in the Middle Ages, but eventually that system came to an end. Further, we do not need to go back seven hundred years to make this point. For the longest time it has been a dearly held belief of many in America that individual freedom and capitalism go together as happy and mutually dependent partners. Freedom facilitates capitalism, and capitalism facilitates freedom.

As with so many cherished tenets in the history of political and social philosophy, this convenient understanding of the situation has been overtaken by actual events. The rise of China has rather put the lie to this: the authoritarian capitalism that one sees there indicates quite clearly that market capitalism can go hand in hand with totalitarianism. In the first chapter, I commented that the tragedy of the Left was that its intellectuals thought the working classes wanted political influence, whereas what they really seem to have desired was satellite televisions and consumer goods. The same is true, in a way, on the Right, if the China pattern is anything to go by. The students of 1989 wanted political freedom, but the people were given consumerism, with its automobiles, computers, and designer clothes, and this seems to have been an alternative that, at least from the outside perspective, preempted any Berlin Wall-style collapse of the Communist regime there. By all means, be a capitalist in the present time—there is no other option—but be aware that to make it *the* Christian system or to connect it inextricably to individual freedom is to make an unverifiable and rather sweeping assertion, and one that seems increasingly problematic.

In fact, there are many things about capitalism of which Christians should be wary. First, it can focus minds on economic prosperity in a way that is not biblical. Nobody wants to be poor—I certainly do not. There is no virtue in poverty considered in itself. But we need to be careful about simplistically identifying either wealth with divine blessing or the impact of the gospel with economic prosperity. Neither is biblical. The story of Job makes it clear that there is no mechanistic connection between being right with God and enjoying earthly, material bounty. The life of Paul speaks to precisely the same thing. To read of his sufferings in the book of Acts, or his own description of his ministry, especially in 2 Corinthians, is to enter a world where it is not wealth and ease but rather hardship and poverty that flow from his fidelity to the cross. Indeed, in 1 Corinthians the very logic of the cross in chapters

1 and 2 would seem to militate against any identification of the gospel with necessary prosperity.

Further, there are other hints in the Bible that the arrival of the good news is sometimes very bad news for the economy. In Mark 5, Jesus exorcises the poor man, Legion, who has presumably been making life in his town a misery for the inhabitants, with his dangerous behavior, his screams that tear up the silence of the night, and the general unpleasantness of having a man possessed by countless demons running wild in the neighborhood. Yet at the end of the story, the people beg Jesus to go. Why? Well, we know that the Decapolis was an area of high Gentile/Roman population, and the huge herd of pigs in the story would indicate that the pork trade was a major plank of the local economy. Jesus' action had put that economy into the tank. That seems to be the only reason one can infer from the text as to why the man who had liberated the town from such nasty and antisocial behavior would be asked to leave. The gospel came to the Decapolis; the economy disappeared down the toilet.

As I said above, all this is emphatically not to argue that prosperity is a bad thing; it is rather to state the biblically obvious fact that there is no necessary connection between biblical faithfulness and God's blessing on the one hand, and material prosperity and economic boom times on the other.

Christians also need to be aware that capitalism does not necessarily foster the kind of behavior, outlook, and ethics that Christians themselves prize. The notion that capitalism produces personal responsibility, initiative, innovation, and strong families is a prevalent one in some quarters; but regardless of whether each of these points is true, there is another side to capitalism that is not so conducive to Christianity.

Think, for example, of the central dynamic of the modern Western economy—consumerism. Consumerism depends on a variety of dispositions among consumers for its success; and indeed, it works hard at cultivating and reinforcing these. For a start, it requires dissatisfaction with the present and with current possessions. After all, if I am perfectly happy with those bell-bottom jeans, tie-dyed shirts, and platform shoes I bought in 1979, I am not going to replace them with a more up-to-date wardrobe, and those who make jeans, shirts, and shoes are going to lose a customer, and, worst-case scenario, possibly go out of business. Thus the manufacturers need to make me dissatisfied with what I have, through commercials, through influencing fashion, through telling me that, hey, the life you have now could be so much better if you traded in the Mott the Hoople gear for something designed more recently by Ralph Lauren. Notice what is going on here: dissatisfaction is being cultivated as a necessary part of keeping the capitalist system ticking over.

Now, let me go on record and say that I am happy enough not to be walking around, looking like an extra for a low-budget movie about Elton John's early career; I enjoy having nice, new things and not being stared at for all the wrong reasons as I walk down my street. My point is rather this: be aware that not all the effects of capitalism are unconditional goods, consistent with the gospel and with the Christian mind-set; we need to be as self-aware of the impact of this way of life as that of any other.

There are other elements of capitalism that are scarcely Christian in their essence. Certainly, as it has developed since the 1970s, capitalism, aka consumerism, has tended to make conspicuous consumption and acquisition of things into a good.

Again, consumerism is good to the extent that it drives our economies and helps in the creation of wealth; but it is always going to tend toward the message that the meaning of life is found in the accumulation of property—a vain exercise, as the Preacher makes clear in Ecclesiastes 2. This is simply another form of idolatry—an ascribing of divine power to things that in themselves do not possess such power, and, we might add, that can be done to systems such as capitalism just as easily as possessions such as golf clubs.

Yet there are more problems, more temptations associated with this ethos. I have already mentioned commercials and advertisements that are essentially designed to make one dissatisfied with one's life and propose further purchases as the solution. But the problem is not simply the gospel of salvation by consumption that they preach; it is also the idea that I am in control of my own destiny, that I hold the answer to my problems, that this lies in the creaturely realm. I can buy this thing, go to that place, spend my money here, and thereby solve my dissatisfaction or reinvent myself or simply make life more pleasant and a whole lot easier. The problem with that message is that it effectively cons me into thinking I am a god; I can do it. It is a form of Pelagianism, built on the idea that I am my own god who can work the miracle of my own happiness by what I do with my cash.

This also helps to cultivate the fixation on individual rights, which, as I commented in chapter 2, afflicts Right as well as Left. In a world where I am the one who determines my own destiny by deciding what I will and will not buy, and where rugged individualism is so deeply ingrained in the culture, then church discipline goes out the window. Discipline me today, and next Sunday I simply give my (spiritual) business to another church (store). That is as consistent a consumerist (and secular) ethic as it is possible to imagine; it pervades and cripples our churches, and it lies at the very heart of the system of social organization that we exalt as being somehow more Christian than previous options.

More sinister still is that to which I have alluded above—the ability of capitalism to remake not simply social relations but social values as well. In a world where the consumer is king, ultimately taste and profit margins will triumph. Much consumption is built on aesthetics, most obviously in issues relating to fashion, but more subtly in a host of other areas. A message that has at its core the idea that the individual is free, self-determining, even self-creating is inevitably antithetical to any idea that there should be external limits placed on that individual. To impose such limits is distasteful because they offend the individualist sensibilities of the consumer society. My father's generation would no doubt have tried to make arguments concerning "the good of society," but these now carry little weight: why is the good of society enhanced by the limiting of the individual? Indeed, what is "society" other than the arbitrary construction of a powerful group of individuals?

Further, deep down inside, the consumer society teaches us all to believe that it is individual consumption that is good for everyone, because that creates wealth, enhances our standards of living, and makes us feel better about ourselves. From a pure propaganda point of view, this is a good move: greed is good because, actually, it helps everyone; I can therefore indulge in it as an act of altruism.

Following on from this is the role that finance plays in shaping ethical decisions. I for one am very uncomfortable with those who use arguments based on economic prosperity, even as one of their subsidiary arguments, to protect the family against such things as abortion and weakening divorce laws. If you start down the path of using the logic of the marketplace to defend traditional moral positions, you leave yourself hopelessly vulnerable when someone comes along who can either refute your economic data or propose something that solves the economic problem.

Increasingly, we see free-market logic being used in moral issues. I noted above the concern that anti-gay-marriage legislation might be damaging to the economy in California. It should be disappointing to those on both sides of the issue that such pure pragmatism now has a role in debating such an important moral issue. No doubt we are all also familiar with arguments regarding drugs, prostitution, and pornography that have similar economic, or supply-and-demand, logic attached to them. And what about end-of-life care for the very old? Arguments for euthanasia? And for abortion as a means of lowering welfare costs? It is hard to imagine a premodern society where child-bearing was seen as a burden or, given that age was valued for its wisdom and for its lifetime of contribution, where people would have had serious discussions about whether it was worth looking after the aged. But in an advanced capitalist society, unwanted babies look dangerously like unproductive appetites and old age speaks of lack of energy and innovation, and, frankly, lack of ability to produce wealth. Of what use are such people? This is not to say that capitalism leads to euthanasia, but it creates one of the kinds of societies where such discussion might well take place. A world that revolves around consumerism and technology inevitably favors youth as those with the energy and flexibility to capitalize on the historical moment.

Old age may seem a long way off to readers under the age of forty, but there are other issues that pinch at a younger age. Conservative Christians often decry the fact that stay-at-home mothers seem less valued than they once were, and the working mom is now the norm. Well, what do you expect from a society where the ability to contribute directly to the wealth-creation process is ultimately the measure of somebody's social standing and value? If the inability to produce children was a sign of a woman's inferiority in premodern society, so the inability to bring home a paycheck is similar today. Christians must realize that capitalism has brought great goods in its wake; but it is not an unmixed blessing, and some of the things about which Christians become most hot under the collar, from the reshaping of the family to the ease of access to abortion, are not unconnected to the system that they often admire with so little critical reflection.

Indeed, the commitment to the capitalist ethic of so many with traditional values regarding family, education, etc., is fascinating. It is clear that as the world moved from feudalism to economies based on trade and production, values changed, and even the family was restructured as people moved from rural areas to cities and family units became smaller. There are other less obvious areas of impact. Many Christian families want to instill a love of great literature in their children; but think of how modern capitalism connects to the entertainment industry, of how even the imagination has been turned into a marketable commodity, with Disney turning classics such as *Notre Dame de Paris* into sentimental, marketable pap; and children's minds being more full of the exciting whizbangs of the movies and the countless spin-off toys, than of the somewhat more ponderous exercise of reading. This is capitalism at work: it has its great benefits, but it has a side to it that is inimical to traditional Christian values and aspirations, and we need to understand and acknowledge it before we promote it as an unconditional good or panacea.

At heart, the problem of contemporary capitalism is that its (at least theoretical) commitment to untrammeled markets as providing the best mechanisms for the shaping of life leads inexorably toward a form of libertarianism—economic at the outset but profoundly moral in the long run. And no economic system, least of all perhaps capitalism, can long survive without some kind of larger moral underpinning that stands prior to and independent of the kinds of values the market itself generates. How that is to be achieved is, of course, quite another matter; but the answer cannot be found simply within "the morality of the market" because, taken by itself, the market has no morality other than what is generated by the need to turn a profit.

I have already said this several times in this chapter: as far as capitalism goes, there is currently no alternative. But let us not engage in the idolatry of assuming that the capitalist way is God's way in any absolute sense. It brings much good in its wake, not least the creation of wealth and the facilitation of social mobility, but it is not an unmixed blessing. It promotes a view of life rooted in material accumulation; it can tend to drive all social relations and values to being determined by cash transactions; and when given spiritual significance, it can become something that looks a little too much like the prosperity gospel. Prosperity is a good thing, as are democracy, good food, and shops that sell clothes that don't appear to have been designed for Elton John, but it is not the gospel. Let's not make that confusion.

RULERS OF THE
QUEEN'S NAVEE

DEMOCRACY: NOT A PLACE FOR PRECISION

Among many traditional, Reformed, confessional, and conservative evangelicals, there has been an understandable reaction in recent years against the kind of theological proposals coming out of movements such as the emergent church and, closer to home, the Federal Vision. Debates with these groups have taken place on a whole variety of fronts, but one of the central bones of contention has been theological precision. Particularly within the ranks of the emergents there has been a reaction against the idea of theological precision, on the ground that the use of precise terminology often claims too much certainty or, to use the cliché, puts God into a box. Against this, many more-traditional theological churches have argued that such precision, far from endangering biblical fidelity, is in fact vital to it and that the church developed precise theological concepts and terms because the proclamation of God's truth in fidelity to the Bible actually demands such precision.

I do not want to address that issue here, but I do want to highlight an interesting phenomenon: while conservative theological types (among whom I number myself) are often very concerned about theological precision, we can tend to think in rather simplistic, black-and-white, clichéd terms when it comes to politics. Indeed, if I had a dollar for every conversation that told me, in blanket terms, that all liberals are guilty of sin x or policy y or think along the lines laid out in z, I would be a rich man. Lest I appear to be slapping only the Right, I have noticed the same kind of lack of nuance on the Left, particularly among those younger evangelicals who like to play the "We voted Democrat, aren't we naughty?" card.

This phenomenon raises an interesting question: Why do those who have a great capacity for subtle thinking in matters of theology seem to prefer to think in terms of very straightforward, black-and-white, if not Manichaean, categories when it comes to politics? I can offer no definitive answer, but I want in this essay to make a few suggestions.

It is important to note at the outset that there is a strange anomaly at the very heart of the democratic process in representative democracies, where the legislative body is not the entire population but rather a very small number of men and women appointed by the whole to represent the whole. This has a host of implications, but one of the most important is the way it requires simplification and destruction of nuance by the very process required to make it work.

Politics is complicated. It covers a host of issues relating to human life, which itself is a very complex phenomenon. Thus it speaks to economics, to foreign policy, to social and personal ethics, to the connection between the nation as a whole and the regions considered individually, to defense, to health care. You name it, politics speaks to it, even if only to say "leave it alone." Then, within each of these subdivisions of political science, there are numerous further complexities. Indeed, despite efforts to the contrary, such as Marxism, there does not appear to be a grand, unifying theory in politics that allows all these areas to be tied together into one coherent and necessary whole. The relationship between particular views of economics and, say, local social policy is often not a necessary one. Even Marxism, perhaps the most obvious example of a school that has attempted to produce a single, all-embracing political view of the world, proved utterly fragmentary, with almost as many denominations in its heyday as Protestantism. The bottom line seems to be that politics as a whole is an art, not a science, and that individual political philosophies are generally eclectic.

The problem with this basic premise is, of course, that as soon as somebody enters the voting booth, all this goes out the window. There, the voter is faced with a set of boxes, perhaps as few as two, and the responsibility to put a mark in one box and not the others. Representative democratic politics, particularly as it plays out in the party system with which most democracies operate, is not conducive to subtlety. Indeed, it is absolutely antithetical to subtlety. It is rather like that scene in the movie where Indiana Jones is confronted by a sword-wielding assassin who stands in front of him, demonstrating his balletic brilliance with a sword. The impatient Jones, having endured the display for a few seconds, merely draws his pistol and shoots the man dead. Every individual issue has its complexities and subtleties; but when you go into the voting booth, you cannot grapple with all of these; you have one bullet and you make it count.

On one level, this is just a fact of democratic life. To paraphrase Winston Churchill, democracy is a bad system, but it is better than any of the others that have been tried. It may not be perfect, but who of us would choose to live under a Hitler, or a Stalin, or even a Franco? And partisan politics, too, would seem relatively desirable. For politicians, the party system provides a good context for organizing campaigns and pooling resources. It also makes governing possible, since the party system imposes a certain coherence on the whole process: trade-offs, coalitions, party-line voting all help to get the business of running a state done with a degree of efficiency. Indeed, looked at in this light, the fact that many major democracies have, in effect, a two-party system is also an advantage: while it limits choice, it also limits the capacity for chaos. Very few citizens in the USA would probably wish to change places with those from countries with a record of regular coalition governments, where the balance of power can be held by a small minority party with some odd distinctive as its central platform.

On another level, however, this disconnect between the complexity of politics and the simplistic nature of democratic voting becomes a problem when we invert the order, and allow the crude restrictions of the ballot box to dominate the way we think about the various political issues that press in on us at any given time. We need to be very wary of developing the mentality of Gilbert and Sullivan's Rt. Hon. Joseph Porter, K.C.B., in *H.M.S. Pinafore*:

> I grew so rich that I was sent
> By a pocket borough into Parliament.
> I always voted at my party's call,
> And I never thought of thinking for myself at all.
> I thought so little, they rewarded me
> By making me the Ruler of the Queen's Navee![1]

The fictional Sir Joseph was, of course, a partisan politician and was thus expected, by and large, not to think for himself but merely to vote as and when his party requested; but as citizens, we surely need to set the bar higher and not allow *a priori* partisanship to trump our political thinking. Christians in particular need to set good examples of civic engagement; and that requires that we take our civic duties seriously, and spend time thinking through complex issues in a way that allows us to act in an informed and intelligent manner. Indeed, I would suggest that all Christians should vote, as part of their civic duty, but they should also feel pain when they mark the relevant box, knowing the trade-offs they are having to make as they do so, and how their action belies the complexity of reality.

THE RISE OF AESTHETICS AND THE DECLINE OF DISCOURSE

Of course, it is not that simple, because there are plenty of other cultural forces, in addition to the ballot box, designed to short-circuit thoughtful engagement with the political process. One oft-cited watershed in political history is the presidential debate between Richard Nixon and John F. Kennedy in 1960, where the

1. http://www.victorianweb.org/mt/gilbert/porter.html. Accessed 3/15/2010.

TV audience thought Kennedy won, but those listening on the radio gave the decision to Nixon. The reason would appear to be the aesthetic appeal of a youthful, tanned Kennedy sitting opposite a rather haggard and tired Nixon, recently released from a hospital. If this was not the birth of the modern age in political campaigning, it certainly stands as the point where the new rules became obvious: appearance was more important than argument.

In the half-century since that debate, the prioritizing of aesthetics has only become more important. Campaigns involve the spending of vast sums of money, much of it on television commercials, where little in the way of argument is served up, the focus rather being on the brightly colored, smiling pictures of the favored candidate, juxtaposed to the sepia or even black-and-white shots of the opponent looking surly or shifty or preferably both. Looking good is now almost at the level of possessing a pulse and a checkbook for the political hopeful. Indeed, it is hard to imagine a political party choosing as its leader a man like Michael Foot, who led the British Labour Party from 1980 to 1983, complete with donkey jacket, homemade haircut, and 1940s glasses. Gordon Brown, the last Labour Prime Minister, is a man known for his morose demeanor and his crooked, stained teeth—until, that is, the months leading up to his taking over from Tony Blair, when the teeth miraculously straightened and became somewhat whiter, and a rather unconvincing smile started to appear on his face, as muscles unused for years suddenly started kicking into action to make him more electable.

Life is so dominated by visual media that such developments were, in retrospect, inevitable, particularly in places such as the USA. Way back in the 1930s, the English writer George Orwell commented on the fact that there were no pictures of ugly people in the typical American magazine. That applies in much the same way to American television today. Soap operas, movies, dramas are all populated by specimens of beauty. There is simply no equivalent of the rather kitchen-sink type dramas that one finds in Britain, where, in soaps such as *Eastenders* and *Coronation Street*, the possession of good looks, a complete set of teeth, and a vaguely attractive personality are completely optional. Indeed, in America one could be forgiven for thinking that if a woman just fails to make the grade as a supermodel, then she becomes a weathergirl as a Plan B.

What this does in the political world is take attention away from substantial issues and focus them on matters of aesthetics and appearance. Good looks backed up by a plausible sound bite will beat any sophisticated argument coming out of a face with a squint, crooked teeth, and pockmarks any day. It is not what is said so much as who is saying it and how the person is saying it that counts. The most brazen example of this aesthetic triumph is in the farcical candidate debates that now take place before a presidential election.

The rules of these encounters are that each candidate has two minutes to answer a question, and the opponent has one minute to offer a rebuttal. The moderator can, at his or her discretion, allow an extra thirty seconds for each. This raises an obvious question: What kind of subject can be satisfactorily debated under such time limits without massive oversimplification of the issues involved? Clearly, only something of the level of "Do you think cowboy boots are best made of cowhide or ostrich skin?" Anything more substantial is going to take considerably longer. Thus it is clear that the debates are not really meant to be debates at all; they are rather vaudeville sketches that allow the players to make their pitch for public affection or support, rather like those balloon debates at school: "I don't think I should be thrown out of the balloon because my mother makes the best cookies!"

A great example of this is surely the first presidential debate of 2000, between Al Gore and George W. Bush. Gore just did not understand the medium, offering statistics and attempts at argument. Bush's responses were folksy; he mocked Gore's use of statistics as "fuzzy math," but he did offer some of his own. The difference was that Bush embedded his statistics in the context of a storyline about families, hitting the kind of emotional chord that works and that trumps pure argument every time. Gore looked like a pompous windbag (not something that required huge effort or genius on his part), and while Bush had little substance, that did not matter. Democracy had come to this: a man incapable of expressing himself succinctly versus a man who saw that there was no real need to put together an argument when a few funny put-downs and some good story lines would work much better.

NEVER MIND THE ARGUMENT, TELL ME A GOOD STORY

This highlights one other aspect of the kind of culture in which we live, where the televisual medium is so dominant: stories are better than facts, logic, and old-style argument. Stories, of course, carry huge power. This is surely part of the reason for the otherwise incomprehensible popularity of country-and-western music. The church should also appreciate this; after all, to state the obvious, the Bible contains many stories; and the church has always produced histories in order to inspire, encourage, and, on occasion, warn its people. It is part of all cultures, and America is no exception. Indeed, many of the buzzwords of American politics—*patriotism, liberty,* even the adjectives *American* and *un-American*—are the linguistic property of all sides in the political debate, with meanings determined largely by the stories the various factions choose to give them context. For example, for some, patriotism means upholding a radical separation of church and state; for others, it involves maintaining Christian values in society. Both views are frequently linked to narratives of the nation's founding—a point reinforced in current politics by the continuing role of the Constitution in American public life.

Stories have thus had huge political significance in America. Think of the civil-rights struggle, and how tales of lynchings, bombings, marches, and accounts of bus boycotts and desegregating schools inspired people in the past and continue to do so today. Indeed, a significant part of the political arsenal of the gay-rights culture is rooted in being able to make a connection between the situation of blacks under segregation and gays in the contemporary world. Such a connection may well be contrived—I am hard-pressed, for example, to think of anywhere that there has been a need to encourage gay people to register to vote because of widespread threat to prevent their doing so—but it is nonetheless powerful; that is, after all, why they spend so much time playing on it.

Indeed, the role of stories has cut both ways. It is surely the case that the positive portrayal—in soap operas, movies, and sitcoms—of those pursuing particular sexual lifestyles that are antithetical both to the Bible's teaching and to traditional morality has had a more profound impact on how people think about these things than any argument. And other stories of prejudice and persecution, however rare such phenomena might be, also have a deep effect. This is why a murder that is a "hate crime" is now seen in law as more heinous than a random killing: the victims in both may be dead, but society has decided to give the death (and therefore the life) of one more significance than the other because of the grand story into which the crime is fitted. In these areas, the gurus of the New Left have been able to use the media very much to their advantage as a way of bolstering the often silly identity politics of their causes. But it also works on the Right. This is why there has been so much judicial blood spilled over the last few years regarding the teaching of history in public schools, and why passions run so deep on both sides of the various debates on this matter: those who control the stories, so the thinking goes, can control the way people think about the world.

Think of the heart of much conservative American identity, where rugged individualism, the frontier, the family, and the ideal of the loner are so significant. Indeed, was there ever a more quintessentially conservative medium than the cinematic Western where, in *Shane*, *The Searchers*, and *High Noon*, these kinds of elements provide the staple of the story lines? The same also play strongly in the political landscape of the Right today. The last presidential election provided some classic examples. The description of McCain and Palin as "the original mavericks" was interesting. The description was clearly absurd. To gain the party's nomination, McCain had obviously had to broker all kinds of agreements and, presumably, make all kinds of promises to the various constituencies that held influence. In other words, whatever his maverick past, that was not going to help him now, other than as a marketing ploy.

Then it should surely be obvious that, logically speaking, the idea of electing a maverick as president should surely not be that appealing. The president has to be someone who can make deals, who leads in such a way that people—Congress, the armed forces, etc.—will respect him and follow. These are not generally the kinds of skills associated with those who do that "mavericky" thing—whatever that may be, given that it remained somewhat undefined during the election. But it worked; it proved hugely popular on the Right because it is consonant with the kind of story the Right likes to tell about itself—rugged, lonely, frontier-type language. One could add to this the other bits and bobs that Sarah Palin threw into the mix: hockey mom, Washington outsider, etc. They worked because they meant something within the narrative. The fact that she was unable in a television interview to define the "Bush doctrine" and was taken apart in another by Katie Couric—the equivalent of being savaged to death on live television by a teddy bear (not a particularly "mavericky" moment, I would guess)—did not seem to dent her appeal with conservative voters. Her competence was determined by her ability to play to the images and the story line, not to handle the policy issues with any degree of confidence. This she has continued to do with some success since the election, with her blogs continuing to be heavy on populist appeal and short on facts and argument.

The flip side of this is the way in which a dominant narrative can be so powerful in the minds of some that it creates odd (or, to use Bushese, perhaps "fuzzy") logic and effectively relativizes awkward facts and events. The most obvious is the way liberals and conservatives often flip-flop on whether big government is good or bad. It is a mantra of the Left that the federal government needs to take a larger role at home, where, apparently, it can and should be trusted; but in foreign policy, the Left's wisdom is that it can do almost nothing of any moral probity. On the Right, however, there is deep suspicion of the federal government in a domestic context; but invade somebody else's country, and any criticism of the government is decried as unpatriotic and un-American. How can these things be? One plausible explanation is that the logic of Left and Right is shaped more by some form of story, which does not conform to normal rules of logical analysis, but which nonetheless carries power for the true believer. Thus the Left has bought into a narrative that says that poverty can be alleviated only by curbing the power of big-business exploitation and by wealth redistribution, but that foreign wars are only ever motivated by the greed of the same big-business concerns that are the problem at home. The Right, however, sees growth of domestic government as inhibiting freedom on the domestic front but as exporting democracy on the international stage.

This kind of culture may well explain some other examples of inconsistency. One example is the avoidance of service in Vietnam by Bill Clinton—something used by his opponents to try to derail his presidential bid. This was consistent with the established conservative narrative of yellow-bellied, liberal draft-dodgers. Then along comes George W. Bush with a Vietnam record that is not exactly above suspicion and with more than a whiff of elite string-pulling about it. This was hardly in line with the conservative narrative— hints of draft-dodging and special privilege being, one would have thought, a lethal combination—but it did minimal damage to his core support; and with equal doses of irony and sleaze, Bush's campaign in 2000, of course, infamously "tolerated" a smear campaign against a genuine war hero, John McCain. Strange to tell, the same people who were so incensed by Clinton's draft-dodging seemed to give Bush a pass. Then, in 2004, along came John Kerry, this time a liberal with what seems to have been a solid Vietnam record. This definitely did not fit the narrative—a liberal of considerable personal bravery and solid military credentials—and we then have all the Swift boat veterans palaver. To describe this flip-flopping as totally bizarre would seem to be an understatement; and it hardly speaks well of the Right's consistency, let alone the moral integrity of those who, for example, engaged in the smears against McCain and Kerry; but the dominant story was so strong that the occasional anomalous and pesky fact was pretty impotent to change it in any fundamental way.

IT'S NOT THE ECONOMY, IT'S CHARACTER AND RHETORIC, STUPID!

This highlights one further aspect of the storytelling nature of much contemporary political engagement: the battle over politics has so often become a battle over character. If you can bear to do it, sit and watch a few political-campaign commercials. Often, unless a litmus issue such as abortion is mentioned, it can be difficult to tell to which party the candidate (or, in a negative ad, the target) belongs, because so little time is spent on substantive policy issues and so much is focused on alleged personal virtues or vices, as revealed by some life event or action—a happy family, a bad decision in a court case, a problem on a tax return, a video of the candidate helping an old lady cross the road/pushing old lady under a van, etc. In a world where political argument is all about stories, character is king; the problem being, of course, that character never necessarily implies competence for any of the job's technical policy aspects.[2]

One might add to this the language that often occurs on conservative talk radio and elsewhere about "elites"—whether Washington, Hollywood, law schools, or whatever. Indeed, while *elite* may in many contexts be a good word—does anyone, for example, want a less-than-elite brain surgeon to open his or her skull?—in political discourse on the Right it is used rather like the dreaded black spot of the pirates in *Treasure Island*. Just as in Britain the language of class always elicits a visceral reaction from the Left, even when on the lips of a socialist as quintessentially upper-class as Tony Benn, so use of the *e* word on the Right in America has much the same effect on its core constituency. When this card was played by George Bush, the irony is, of course, that there is no one more elite than President Bush, as his Vietnam record implies. The son of a former president, he might play the "I'm just a good old boy from Texas" line; but make no mistake, he is as elite as they come. Again, let me emphasize, I am not making a party political point here; I am simply indicating that politics in the present age is not ultimately about policies, because that would require arguments. It is really about images—visual and narrative. As in Britain, there is a class narrative where "they"—the upper class—have historically always had it in for the rest of us. So in America there is a narrative that "they"—the liberal coastal elites—have always

2. It might also be a function of a world where actual policy differences between parties have become so small that there is need for other forms of discriminating between the various options, but that is a story for another day.

worked to undermine American values. Even when this tale is told by someone as obviously elite as George Bush, it retains power precisely because he knows which buttons to press. Tell people a story about the "elites" that they want to hear, and they will listen, even if you are really opposed to their interests. Give them an argument, backed up by statistics, and you will sound like an "elite" yourself; and they will turn away in boredom, even if what you have to tell them would be to their advantage.

The power of stories also goes a long way in helping to explain the strange networks and alliances of beliefs that often exist in the political mind-set. For example, I wonder how many on the Left have ever taken the time to address the issue of how the right to abortion became so inextricably linked to the notion of women's rights. Or how the Left, which prides itself on speaking up for those who cannot speak up for themselves, has in modern America almost universally made the right to choose the litmus test of whether one is truly politically liberal or not. Not by scientific argument based on genetics, or even on the age at which a fetus is viable outside the womb—it has been done primarily on an emotive story about the oppression of women, which focuses on the individual as the only person who really matters in each particular narrative. In this story, the fetuses are not persons and thus do not qualify as those who cannot speak up for themselves and thereby merit the patronage of the Left.

The Right, too, pulls similar tricks. While much of the political rhetoric in conservative religious circles focuses on abortion, one never has to scratch too far below the surface to find that a host of other, biblically somewhat more ambiguous, issues are susceptible to the same black-and-white, Christians-believe-this, godless-liberals-believe-that rhetoric. Gun control is one such issue. There are surely arguments to be made on both sides of this equation, and there is also a debate to be had as to whether one-size-fits-all legislation is appropriate for places as diverse in terms of social issues as Philadelphia and Billings. What is interesting is that the position of the Right on this is often rooted in a particular narrative of how "they"—the Left, the federal government, etc.—operate. Several times I have heard the argument that if the right to bear arms is restricted today, "they'll be locking us up without trial tomorrow." Worldwide, there is very little evidence that these two phenomena are inevitably, necessarily, and causally linked. But in a narrative going right back to the founding of America in 1776, there is a strong rhetorical connection that seems almost impossible to break, mainly because arguments against it are just that—arguments—and not the kind of gripping narratives that really drive so many beliefs and convictions.

Health care might provide another example: it is not obvious to me from reading Scripture that God really cares one way or the other about how health care is delivered. Sickness is a result of the fall. As it was part of God's own character revealed in Christ to reach out with compassion to those ill and suffering, so it should be part of the character of God reflected in Christians to act in a manner consistent with this. I would suggest it means that believers should consider health care a good thing and want to see as many people helped by it as possible. How that is done, to what extent the state is involved, etc., are legitimate subjects for debate and not something that should divide Christians as Christians.

In this context, Sarah Palin's reference to "death panels" is a great example of story trumping logic. It was a flourish of rhetoric with no evidence to support it, and the logic was skewed. The thought of the government 's deciding which old people live and which die is a scary one, and it plays directly into that overarching conservative narrative whereby the government can do no good at home and is an enemy of freedom (despite the fact that the Right generally regards it as the great agent of freedom when it operates abroad). In such a context, she did not need to provide logical argument, merely to hit the typical notes that resonate with the accepted story line.

The truth about health care is that, however much money is available, it will never be enough; all health systems everywhere have to prioritize resources—financial and otherwise—and tough decisions are going to have to be made somewhere down the line. But is investing this power in a democratically elected government really worse than investing it in private insurance companies that decide which claims to honor and which to refuse? Or which preexisting conditions to accept and which to reject? Do these not have the same effect as Palin's mythological death panels? At least with the government, one has the chance, however slim, of throwing them out of office once in a while. As to arguments about efficiency, there are interesting questions to ask about how much of private premiums are spent on advertising. National health systems are not perfect, but they are far from the nightmares that have been depicted in some recent discussions about the USA; and indeed, when only one country in the entire industrialized world does not have some form of universal health care, it may just be that such systems have actually proved rather popular with the majority of the democratic world's people precisely because they have proved compatible with political freedom and quite capable of delivering decent service.

Even more bizarre than the way the health care debate is played out in some quarters is the whole issue of global warming. Now, one assumes that, whatever the complexities of the case, ultimately the impact or not of human-made pollution on the world climate will be a question of empirical fact: it either is or is not true. We may not yet be in a position to determine the status of that question, but hopefully we will be able to do so at some point.

Yet in recent years, I have heard climate change referred to as a "religion" and as a "liberal conspiracy." This is interesting, partly on the grounds that it represents a strange disconnection of the creation mandate from notions of environmental stewardship. While conservative Christians often apply the mandate to all manner of things—from developing Christian approaches to art and movies right through to the production of school curricula that focus on classical languages (as an aside, this may well be an interesting Renaissance idea, but it is scarcely a distinctively Christian one)—those same Christians seem reluctant, even hostile, with regard to any application of the notion to care for the environment. Again, one suspects that this is at least in part the result of what one might call the sheer power of the Great Liberal Conspiracy Narrative, as promulgated on a myriad of talk-radio shows, whereby the fact that certain liberal figures believe it to be taking place is enough in and of itself to discredit the whole idea of climate change and to demand that we look below the surface to find out what the real agenda might be. But that's liberals for you, according to the hard-Right pundits such as Ann Coulter, Glenn Beck, and company—too idiotic to see the truth or to construct a decent argument on anything, but so brilliant that they can mastermind a conspiracy that subverts all aspects of world civilization as we know it.

The fact that Al Gore made a movie about climate change of course does not make it true, but it does not make it false, either. And that said, while the fact that Gore probably flew around the world in a fuel-guzzling jet to promote the movie might speak to issues of personal integrity and consistency, his behavior does not necessarily render his arguments garbage. As noted above, questions of character are limited in terms of usefulness in argument and decision-making; and if that is the case with political philosophy, how much more so with matters that ultimately connect to empirical science. Both sides, of course, are guilty. References on the Left to "climate-change denial" seem little more than a means of subverting argument by creating a rhetorical connection to the phenomenon of Holocaust denial—a lunatic-fringe position if ever there was one—and reference to "the religion of global warming" works in a similar manner on the Right. But why can one not, for example, be convinced by evidence for or against climate change, regardless of one's views on gun control or tax rates? Surely, the responsible citizen will wish to think about each issue on its own merits; and to dismiss climate change as a "liberal position" is to make it the result of a grand conspiracy, and that reflects a mindset where intelligent political discussion simply can no longer take place. Those who (rightly) are often so skeptical of narrative theology might do well to be somewhat skeptical of narrative politics as well; and because narrative politics is virtually the only thing on offer at the moment, that will require an incredible act of will, hard work, and intellectual commitment.

CONCLUSION

To draw all this to a conclusion, it should be clear that I am arguing that democracy as it currently exists addresses very complicated questions, but does so through a system (the party framework) and a culture (televisual and aesthetic) that militate against addressing the issues with the seriousness and subtlety they require. Now, let me say at this point: I am not a utopian. I do not have an alternative setup to offer, but I do believe it is helpful to realize the truth of what I am describing in order that we, as Christians and as citizens, are able to engage both politics and the political process in such a way that we are aware of the problems, limitations, and realistic expectations of what they can deliver. This will not solve the problems, but it may allow us to interact with each other more intelligently and to overcome the rather black-and-white partisanship that so often marks the contributions of Christians to public debates.

I will return to the pragmatic nature of the political process in the final chapter. Suffice it to say at this point that it is crucial that Christians understand the way in which the partisan nature of politics is both polarizing—in that each party has a vested interest in accentuating the differences between the two sides—and subversive of proper thought and discussion, with the increasing dependence on visual, aesthetic, and narrative-type resources instead of argument. These latter simplify issues and create connections between issues (abortion and gun control, for example) that are not logically necessary. To be a good steward in this context requires, therefore, a savvy, critical mind-set that is able to subject the techniques of the party system to appropriate scrutiny.

Above all, though, Christians need to be thoughtful in the way they engage in this area. We should not uncritically buy in to all the story lines that underlie the various political postures being taken out there. Instead, we need to familiarize ourselves with the secular stories being told, and the way in which these shape society and individuals; and we should certainly give no credence to the kind of slapstick populism that is the stock-in-trade of political discourse and that has supplanted argument and logic. No Christian should parade around with a picture of the president as the Joker in *Batman* or associate with those whose idea of an argument is to scream obscenities at elected officials from behind a police barricade. Nor should they adopt the "my party, right or wrong" stance. Political engagement in a democracy inevitably requires engaging with a party, whether as a member or simply as a voter. But as soon as we fall into the trap of assuming that all members or supporters of one party must believe x, y, and z, we are not thinking; we are merely following clichés. The Christian in civic society should set an example to others of what the best citizen looks like, not simply reinforce stereotypes of what the worst appears to be. And that applies across the political spectrum.

CONCLUDING UNPOLITICAL
POSTSCRIPT

THERE IS A SAYING in Britain that usually does the rounds at election time: It doesn't matter for whom you vote, the government will always get in. There is a sense in which this is just a piece of cynicism, indicating a low view of the various parties on offer at any election, but there is also a sense in which it contains a great deal of truth. It is, after all, quite clear that governments in democracies very rarely make the kind of difference that their own electoral pitch would imply; indeed, it is quite remarkable that both radical Right and radical Left candidates tend, once in power, to move toward the center.

There are various reasons for this. First, it is the result of the competitive electoral process, where differences need to be emphasized by all participants in order to make the various party platforms and candidates distinctive. Even now in British politics, when old-style socialism, focused on the notion of a mixed economy and nationalization of utilities, is basically dead, and the main tenets of the free market are embraced by all but the fringe, it is crucial that Labour and Conservative portray themselves as opposites. We may not have quite the rhetoric of Winston Churchill, who infamously claimed in 1945 that it would take the Gestapo to implement Labour's plans (he lost that election, by the way), but hints that social and economic Armageddon may be just around the corner are never far from the surface of the typical campaign.

Second, the nature of the democratic process itself imposes limits on radicalism. Elected politicians have various constituencies to whom they need to look: their party, the people who elected them, and the various lobby groups to whom they look for funding. The interests of these groups are rarely, if ever, identical, and this means the daily life of a politician is a calculated balancing of obligations and risks that, generally speaking, prevents moving in too radical a direction, either right or left. The situation for the men at the top—the president, the prime minister, the chancellor—can be even more complicated, because they have to deal with enemies even within their own parties who quite fancy themselves for the top job.

Third, while politicians like to think of themselves as in charge, they are not the only factors in shaping policy. Paid government bureaucracy is, after all, the one element of true stability and continuity in the process. Republicans and Democrats, Labour and Conservative may come and go, but the pen-pushing bureaucrats remain in place. In addition, anyone involved in any organization will know that change is slow, even in relatively small outfits. To change national structures is exponentially more difficult. In other words, the politicians might play up their significance with phrases such as "Yes, we can!" and "Change we can believe in!" but often the ability to change—at least to change quickly—is somewhat less available than those same politicians can afford to acknowledge during a campaign.

All of this leads me to believe that those Christians who participate in the democratic process need to do so with a realistic understanding of what is and is not possible. We are stewards who should do the best we can, not utopians making heaven on earth. Politics is, even at its best, a thoroughly pragmatic business in that it represents the art of the possible. Now, as a Christian, one could take a hard-line purist position, and decide to vote for the politician who represents, in word and deed, only a consistent Christian position on those matters where such positions are identifiable. If that is the case, then I suspect that person is simply never going to vote, since there does not appear to be such a person or party in existence at this time. And if you do not vote, you really have no influence whatsoever. You can sit on the sidelines, hurling brickbats like Waldorf or Statler, but ultimately you have no voice.

Most Christian traditions have not held to this position, with the notable exception of the Reformed Presbyterians, who for many years did not allow members to vote—a conviction shaped by their own history and understanding of the significance of the Solemn League and Covenant of 1643. Thus it would seem that most Christians, when they go into the voting booth, accept that they are going to cast a vote that involves a degree of pragmatism, since the candidate or party for whom they are voting will represent only a portion of the policies and positions they believe are proper and appropriate for a Christian.

This raises the question: Where does one draw the line? Are there issues that represent watersheds on which Christians cannot compromise, even in the electoral booth? Most conservative Christians, at least in America, would answer yes: abortion. The political role of the abortion debate, particularly as it plays out in the two-party system, has made this a watershed for conservative Christians, both Protestant and Catholic.

As I commented earlier in this book, the way the abortion debate developed is odd. Let me explain. Abortion, involving as it does the termination of the life of a child in the womb, would seem to be a classic cause for the Left. The Left, after all, prides itself on speaking up for the oppressed, especially for those who cannot speak up for themselves. Yet on this issue, the Left has been hijacked largely by those who make it a point of honor *not* to speak up for those who cannot speak up for themselves. The rhetorical connection that has been forged between the oppression of women and the denial of on-demand abortion is quite stunning; it possesses precious little, if any, essential, internal logic; and yet it is now a virtual shibboleth of those who regard themselves as progressive. This is the leap of logic that so shocked the Left libertarian intellectual Nat Hentoff, who correctly understood his role as a man of the Left on this issue and ended up being isolated by the very people with whom, on other political issues, he stood shoulder to shoulder.

I am myself pro-life. Contrary to current cultural logic, my politically liberal instincts (concern for the weak) combine with my evangelical commitments (concern for the sanctity of life) to put me in precisely that camp. Nevertheless, I am suspicious of the way in which the abortion debate plays out in the American political arena, where it seems to be something the Right often uses as little more than a means to drum up cheap votes for its candidates. Bush in 2000 was trumpeted as the pro-life candidate in some Christian quarters; and to his credit as president, he did make a stand on partial-birth abortion, although that is hardly a distinctively pro-life position, since many Americans who approve of *Roe v. Wade* are yet appalled by this practice. Yet it would appear that Bush's nominations to the Texas state judiciary actually had a moderating effect on him as governor of Texas and scarcely constituted evidence of a solid pro-life record.[1] Another good example would be John McCain in the 2008 election, whose track record on abortion and statements about it were ambiguous to say the least, yet the pro-life rhetoric became more marked once he needed the votes.

Further, while the Republican Party is often thought of as the party of the pro-lifers, the picture is a whole lot more complicated than such a simple taxonomy would suggest. There are absolute purists, who will settle for nothing less than an immediate ban on all abortions. And there are incrementalists, who realize that political change takes a long time and who thus want to see candidates working toward the eventual goal of a ban, but who see the road to this place as paved with various intermediate stages, such as the lowering of the legal term within which abortion may be carried out and the restriction of legitimate candidates. Then within both groups there are debates about who exactly is a legitimate candidate for the procedure, such as rape victims, mothers whose lives are at risk by pregnancy, etc.

1. Jim Yardley, "Bush's Choices for Court Seen as Moderates," *New York Times*, July 9, 2000, http://www.nytimes.com/2000/07/09/us/bush-s-choices-for-court-seen-as-moderates.html?pagewanted=1 (accessed 3/22/2010).

Given this, a number of thoughts come to mind when reflecting on the abortion debate. First, given the pro-life rhetoric, what is the actual Republican record on abortion like? Not very impressive. The *Roe v. Wade* ruling came down in 1973. Since that time, Republicans have enjoyed the lion's share of the presidency, and have also had periods of significant control of Congress. Yet *Roe* still stands and rates of abortion are catastrophically high, to the extent that the pro-life movement is currently divided over the real pro-life credentials of a conservative president such as George W. Bush, now that he has left office (the rhetoric being somewhat less equivocal in 2000 and 2004). It seems clear that the democratic legislative path to reducing or even outlawing abortions is proving remarkably unfruitful, a fact that may connect to the complexity of getting legislation passed in the American system of checks and balances. Or, more cynically, this may be due to the fact that a majority of Americans are, sadly, in favor of abortion and politicians need their votes to get elected.

Second, and following from this first point, if the democratic legislative path to addressing the issue is proving unfruitful, is there any point in allowing the matter to be the make-or-break issue on which individuals make their voting decisions at election time? Or is it simply a rhetorical game, played by cynical politicians on both sides of the debate to rally their supporters and demonize the opposition? Is the one who votes for the pro-choice Democratic candidate really any more or less culpable on the abortion issue than the one who votes pro-life Republican, knowing that the candidate's rhetoric will in no way be matched by any legislative action? Most pro-life Republicans I know are functionally incrementalists: they vote as pro-life, but know that change, if it happens at all, will happen only slowly. If incremen-talism is acceptable at a macro level, why not at a party level? Is it not acceptable for pro-life Democrats to work with the same incremental strategy and philosophy within their own party to achieve change? Bottom line: abortion will be overturned in the USA only when a majority of people voting for both parties wish to see it happen. Using it as a wedge issue at election time to polar-ize opinion will not achieve that for which Christians all long: the reduction and ultimate elimination of legal abortions.

In one way, this takes us to the heart of politics from a Christian perspective: it is a deeply pragmatic phenomenon at all levels— that of the individual who votes and the candidate who stands. As I mentioned above, the capacity for change, for real change, is always restricted by factors beyond the control of any individual politician; and for this reason, Christians need to see their political responsibilities here and now in terms of good stewardship. You can talk theonomy, theocracy, or Christian nation if you wish, but in the real world of the here and now, Christians have to cast their votes in terms of the situation, as we currently know it. Christians are to be good citizens, as is very clear from New Testament teach-ing on respect for civil authorities; and whatever childish rhetoric about "Marxism" and "Fascism" and "totalitarianism" fills the air, we in America do not live under anything like the oppression Paul endured in the first century, nor like that meted out in truly Marx-ist and Fascist states.

Beyond abortion, there are a whole host of issues on which the Christian pundits have strong opinions, from gun control to defense spending to financial regulation to education. The prob-lem is, of course, that whether there is a distinctly biblical position on these matters that can thus be pressed on the church is debatable. Is it Christian to support spending on arms that may be used in an unjust war? Or is it Christian to oppose arms spending when this might leave the nation vulnerable to attack? You tell me. However, it is simply not the church's job to parse political issues in this way. Certainly, anyone examining the great creedal and confessional statements of the church will draw a blank. The creeds and confessions address the central truths of God and the gospel; and in restricting themselves to this content, they make a point about the church, that it is made up of those who hold to the truth of God's salvation in Christ, not to this or that social policy or political philosophy. Sure, there are basic elements to Christian ethics: respect for life, honesty, care for the poor, etc.; and in preaching the gospel week by week, the church shapes the minds and the ethics of her people; but how these things manifest themselves at the level of political policy is something with which Christians, as members of civic society, have to wrestle and over which they can legitimately disagree.

The danger in taking strong political positions on these issues, and, even worse, partisan politics, is that the church will ultimately exclude those who do indeed believe the gospel and who should therefore be included. As Christians, we should be able to disagree vigorously on, say, gun control. We should, if you like, be able to stand on opposite sides of the protest lines on such issues Monday to Saturday, and yet come together to take the Lord's Supper on Sunday as Christian brothers and sisters united by a common faith, even as we are divided by our strongly held politics.

Christians are to be good citizens, to take their civic responsibilities seriously, and to respect the civil magistrates appointed over us. We also need to acknowledge that the world is a lot more complicated than the pundits of Fox News (or MSNBC) tell us. We must never engage in the kind of inappropriate behavior of those who carry around pictures of our appointed leaders as criminals, or who scream mindless abuse at those with whom they disagree. Christian politics, so often associated now with loudmouthed aggression, needs rather to be an example of thoughtful, informed engagement with the issues and appropriate involvement with the democratic process. And that requires a culture change. We need to read and watch more widely, be as critical of our own favored pundits and narratives as we are of those cherished by our opponents, and seek to be good stewards of the world and of the opportunities therein that God has given to us.

It is my belief that the identification of Christianity, in its practical essence, with very conservative politics will, if left unchallenged and unchecked, drive away a generation of people who are concerned for the poor, for the environment, for foreign-policy issues. Further, as the Right itself shifts distinctly in a more socially and morally libertarian direction, and even on issues such as abortion is shown to be more and more pragmatic in terms of the disconnect between election-year rhetoric and postelection delivery, the Religious Right is likely to find itself increasingly disillusioned and marginal, even in mainstream party politics—banished to the sidelines, where it will simply function as a loud but ultimately inconsequential group. We need to avoid this marginalization of the voice of Christians in politics by realizing the limits of politics and the legitimacy of Christians, disagreeing on a host of actual policies, and by earning a reputation for thoughtful, informed, and measured political involvement. A good reputation with outsiders is, after all, a basic New Testament requirement of church leadership, and that general principle should surely shape the attitude of all Christians in whatever sphere they find themselves. Indeed, I look forward to the day when intelligence and civility, not tiresome clichés, character assassinations, and Manichaean noise, are the hallmarks of Christians as they engage the political process.

I close with a quotation from Vaclav Havel, who truly knew what it was like to live under a Marxist state, and not like the hyperbolic foghorns of Limbaugh and Beck. Here, he captures an attitude that would seem to me to be entirely consistent with the sentiment of Martin Luther, stated so bluntly in the heady Reformation days of 1520, that Christian freedom finds its outworking not in the assertion of our own rights but in the service of others in whatever sphere we are placed:

> Genuine politics—even politics worthy of the name—the only politics I am willing to devote myself to—is simply a matter of serving those around us: serving the community and serving those who will come after us. Its deepest roots are moral because it is a responsibility expressed through action, to and for the whole.[2]

---

2. Vaclav Havel, *Summer Meditations* (New York: Knopf, 1992), 6.